Field Guide
to
Amphibians and Reptiles
of Illinois

Field Guide
to

Amphibians and Reptiles
of Illinois

Christopher A. Phillips
Ronald A. Brandon
Edward O. Moll

Illinois Natural History Survey • Champaign
August 1999
Manual 8

Illinois Natural History Survey, David L. Thomas, Chief
A Division of the Illinois Department of Natural Resources,
Brent Manning, Director

Illinois Natural History Survey
Natural Resources Building
607 East Peabody Drive
Champaign, Illinois 61820

Printed by the authority of the state of Illinois

Editor: Thomas E. Rice

About the authors: Christopher A. Phillips is Associate Research
Scientist and Curator of Amphibians and Reptiles at the Illinois Natural
History Survey, Center for Biodiversity, in Champaign. Ronald A.
Brandon is Professor (Emeritus) of Zoology and Curator of Herpetology
at Southern Illinois University in Carbondale. Edward O. Moll is
Professor (Emeritus) of Zoology at Eastern Illinois University in
Charleston and a member of the Illinois Endangered Species Protection
Board.

Partial funding for the preparation of this guide was provided by the
Bureau of Design and Environment, Illinois Department of Transportation.

ISBN: 1-882932-04-8

Citation:
Phillips, C.A., R.A. Brandon, and E.O. Moll. 1999. Field guide to
amphibians and reptiles of Illinois. Illinois Natural History Survey
Manual 8. 300 pp.

In memory of Phil Smith (1921-1986)

Contents

Foreword

This is the eighth of the manual series of the Illinois Natural History Survey. The first was titled *Fieldbook of Illinois Wild Flowers* and was published in 1936. Subsequent manuals have dealt with shrubs, land snails, mammals, mussels, and, most recently, the northeastern longhorned beetles.

This field guide on the amphibians and reptiles of Illinois is written for those who are not necessarily experts on these groups, but who wish to have an easy-to-use guide in the field. Identifications can be made through use of the keys or through excellent photographs of each species.

One of the goals of this book is to help the reader learn about all 102 species of amphibians and reptiles that live within the boundaries of Illinois. Basic information is presented on their biology and life history, as well as a brief discussion of the species that are listed as threatened or endangered under the state's Endangered Species Protection Act. There is a discussion of declining amphibian populations, particularly the cricket frog, and the effects that highways are having on a number of our amphibians and reptiles. This fits nicely with the section "Geologic and Climatic History of Illinois," which discusses how climatic changes previously had an important impact on species distribution and abundance, but now these changes in species distribution are primarily due to the activities of man. There are also sections on the collecting and keeping of amphibians and reptiles, and on ways to improve their habitats.

It is a particular credit to the authors that in addition to all their other duties they were able to put the time and effort in to develop this excellent manual. Tom Rice did an outstanding job of editing and layout for this publication. Many other staff participated in collections and identifications, and as with most of these endeavors a variety of personnel and resources were needed to bring it to successful fruition.

It is hoped that this Manual will be useful to a wide variety of audiences and that it will further and enhance an appreciation of the amphibians and reptiles found in Illinois. These species are important indicators of the state of our natural habitats in Illinois, and their declines are telling us much about habitat loss and environmental alterations in the state.

David L. Thomas
Chief

Acknowledgments

The idea of an amphibian and reptile guide written for a general audience originated with the Illinois Endangered Species Protection Board. Partial funding for this book was provided by the Bureau of Design and Environment, Illinois Department of Transportation. We would like to thank Lauren Brown of Illinois State University, Gary Casper of the Milwaukee Public Museum, and Tom Johnson of the Missouri Department of Conservation for reviewing the manuscript; the curators and managers of collections for providing data on specimens in their care; and our family and friends for encouragement and support. We would also like to thank Tom Rice for editing and layout, and Charlie Warwick for guiding the product through printing. Figures 3, 5, 6a-b, 7a-b, 10a-b, 11, 14, 15, 16, 19a-b, 20, 21a-b, 22a-b, 24a-b, 25a-b, 26a-b, 27a-b, and 31 were drawn by Mark Sabaj; 2, 9, 23 (bottom), 28a-b, 30a-b, and 32a-b by Alice Prickett; 4, 13a-b, 17b, 23 (top), and 29 by Joseph Leveque; 12a,b,c,d by Thomas Johnson (reprinted with permission of the Missouri Conservation Commission); 18a,b by Jeanne Serb; 8a,b by Ron Brandon; and 17a by Chris Phillips. Range maps were produced by Tom Kompare. Special thanks to the photographers who graciously donated their images, without which this guide would not have been possible.

Introduction

Amphibians and reptiles probably evoke more unwarranted fear
and loathing than any other group of organisms. This may be the
result of the mistaken notions that all are wet and slimy and that
many are dangerous to humans. So much mythology has
developed around amphibians and reptiles, especially snakes, that
it is not easy to separate fact from fancy. A first step in the right
direction is to recognize that herpetologists study two different
groups of animals, the class Amphibia and the class Reptilia,
members of which differ greatly in structure, physiology,
behavior, and ecology. While it is true that many amphibians are
wet and slimy to the touch, reptiles, unless they are in water, are
dry. It is also true that amphibians usually are cool to the touch,
but reptiles, through their basking behavior and heat-managing
adaptations, maintain body temperature as high as our own,
sometimes higher, when they are active. While 4 of the 38
species of snakes (11%) in Illinois are venomous, only the
copperhead is relatively widespread; however, it is found only in
the southern half of the state, and is secretive, shy, and not prone
to bite. The other three have limited distributions and specific
habitat requirements that you can learn, or learn to avoid, as you
like. Indeed, one of the goals of this book is to help you learn
more about all 102 species of amphibians and reptiles that live
within the boundaries of Illinois.

Biology and Life History

Food and Feeding
Most amphibians and reptiles are predators of a wide variety of
other kinds of animals, even of each other. Some are omnivorous
(eat animals and plants), and some are herbivorous (eat only
plants).

Salamanders, both larvae and adults, are generalized predators, eating about any other animal they can capture and swallow,

including fish, insects, crayfish, and snails. Salamander larvae begin life eating tiny, almost microscopic, animals known as plankton. As they grow, they eat larger and larger prey. Aquatic salamanders capture prey by lunging and simultaneously opening the mouth and expanding the throat to draw in a rush of water. Because this method does not work in air, terrestrial salamanders simply grasp worms, insects, slugs, snails, and so forth with their jaws or use their protrusible, sticky tongues to pull prey into their mouths.

Most frog and toad tadpoles scrape algae and bacteria from substrate and filter them from water, or scavenge decaying organic matter. Adults are mostly insectivorous, capturing a variety of insects with their protrusible, sticky tongues.

Among reptiles, snakes and most lizards are strictly predatory, but most turtles are omnivorous. Diet may change with age. For example, juvenile red-eared sliders feed mainly on invertebrates, while adults are largely herbivorous.

Foraging is simple for most turtles. Aquatic individuals swim or walk slowly along the bottom and grasp or bite food with their sharp but toothless jaws. Like salamanders, they can create suction by expanding the throat to draw in detached food. Food too large to be swallowed whole is held in the jaws and torn apart with claws of the front feet. The long-necked snapping turtles and softshell turtles may stalk or lie in ambush for prey, then capture them in a rapid biting and sucking strike. The unique alligator snapping turtle has a wormlike lure on its tongue that entices fish within range of its sharp jaws.

Lizards are chiefly bite-and-grasp predators that simply overpower a variety of invertebrates. Most small snakes, as well as garter snakes, racer, and water snakes, simply capture prey with their jaws and swallow them. Snakes that feed largely on mammals and birds use constriction or venom to subdue prey. The constricting bullsnake, rat snakes, and kingsnakes grasp a small mammal or bird in their jaws, coil around it, and squeeze until it is subdued by suffocation or circulatory failure. The venomous pit vipers (copperhead, cottonmouth, and rattlesnakes) inject venom in a rapid strike, then track their stricken prey through their keen sense of smell made possible by the tongue and vomeronasal organ in the roof of the mouth. The fast-acting venom, produced by modified salivary glands, is injected through a pair of long, hollow fangs that can be folded against the roof of the mouth.

Reproduction

Though most frogs and salamanders reproduce during spring, that's where the similarities end. Frog breeding is a clamorous, raucous affair whereas breeding salamanders are secretive and quiet. Male frogs attract females to breeding sites by species-specific vocalizations. Where many individuals of several frog species call simultaneously, the result can be deafening. Males usually arrive at the breeding site before females. When a male is approached by a gravid female, he climbs on her back and holds on with his forearms around her body (a behavior called amplexus). Sometime thereafter, the female releases eggs into the water and the male fertilizes them by expelling sperm on top of them.

Rather than vocalizing, male salamanders entice females to engage in a ritual courtship behavior through an exchange of chemical cues, or pheromones, produced by specialized glands and released into the water or onto the body. During courtship, the male, except the hellbender, deposits spermatophores (small gelatinous pyramids capped with spermatozoa) and leads the female over them. With her cloaca, she removes spermatozoa, which are stored in a special sac-like structure. The eggs are then fertilized inside the female's body. Rather than producing spermatophores, male hellbenders simply spread spermatozoa (milt) over eggs left in a gravel depression by one or more females.

In the biphasic life history of most amphibians in Illinois, eggs laid in water develop into aquatic larvae that grow and transform into juveniles that resemble adults in body form. In the hellbender, mudpuppy, and lesser siren salamanders, larvae mature without transforming and never leave the water. Woodland salamanders (genus *Plethodon*) bypass the larval stage altogether. They lay eggs on land and embryonic development is modified so that hatchlings resemble adults in body form. The external gills, conspicuous on salamander larvae, are concealed in tadpoles beneath an operculum on each side of the head.

Most Illinois reptiles court and mate in spring or autumn. Fertilization is internal with sperm transferred by one of the paired copulatory organs (hemipenes) in lizards and snakes, or by a penis in turtles. All turtles, lizards, and many snakes in Illinois lay eggs. May and June are peak months for egg laying, and many species lay 2–3 times during the nesting season. While eggs of most Illinois turtles are elliptical with flexible leathery shells, eggs of snapping turtles and softshell turtles are spherical and those of mud, musk, and softshell turtles have hard, brittle shells. Female turtles use their hind feet to excavate a nest hole in mud or sand, and carefully cover it after laying eggs. Lizards and snakes conceal eggs under rocks, in or under logs, in organic debris, or in burrows. Female broadhead and five-lined skinks stay with their eggs throughout incubation in a rare display of reptilian parental care. Kirtland's snake, water snakes, Graham's crayfish snake, queen snake, brown snake, redbelly snake, garter snakes, ribbon snakes, lined snake, smooth earth snake, and pit vipers are all live bearers.

Geologic and Climatic History of Illinois

During the last 20,000 years, the Midwest has experienced glaciation and approximately six major climatic phases that greatly influenced current landforms, soils, stream patterns, and vegetation. This in turn influenced the distributions of amphibians and reptiles. For practical purposes, the modern history of amphibian and reptile distributions in Illinois began when the most recent ice sheet, the Laurentide of the Wisconsin glacial period, began to recede from the Midwest. At that time, approximately 15,000–18,000 years before the present (BP), the northern two-thirds of the region that became Illinois was covered with a thick sheet of ice. Much of the remainder was tundra or boreal spruce-fir forest and probably was devoid of reptiles and amphibians. Approximately 10,000 years BP, the climate warmed further and, over the next several thousand years, birches and pines replaced boreal forest. Little is known about the composition of the herpetofauna during this time. The period from approximately 10,000 to 8,000 years BP was characterized by slightly higher temperatures and higher humidity. Vegetation changed from pines to mesic hardwoods such as oak, elm, maple, and beech. During this period, southern species like the mole salamander, bird-voiced treefrog, cottonmouth, and mud snake occurred farther north than they do currently.

The climate from approximately 8,000 to 6,000 years BP was characterized by higher temperature but low humidity. A combination of oak-hickory forest and tallgrass prairie replaced mesic hardwood forests as the dominant vegetation in much of the state. Species that adapted to the xeric Great Plains and southwestern parts of the continent extended their ranges into Illinsia as the Prairie Peninsula expanded into what is now Illinois. Some of these species, such as the yellow mud turtle and western hognose snake, still occur in the state although their ranges have been reduced greatly.

About 4,000 years BP, the climate changed to its current moderate temperature and humidity, with subsequent decrease in area of prairie as mesic forest once again expanded and oak-hickory forest whittled into the prairie from all sides. The seesaw battle between forest and prairie continued for the next few thousand years, controlled by smaller-scale climatic fluctuations and by fires caused by lightning or set by indigenous peoples. The Natural Divisions of Illinois map (Fig. 1) reflects the distributional responses of amphibians and reptiles to the climatic and geologic histories of the state.

The most recent chapter shaping distributions of amphibians and reptiles, especially in prairie habitats, began as Native Americans were replaced by European settlers who had little interest in maintaining prairie plants through periodic burning, but instead controlled wildfires and broke the prairie sod for agriculture. These settlers drained the extensive prairie marshes

Figure 1

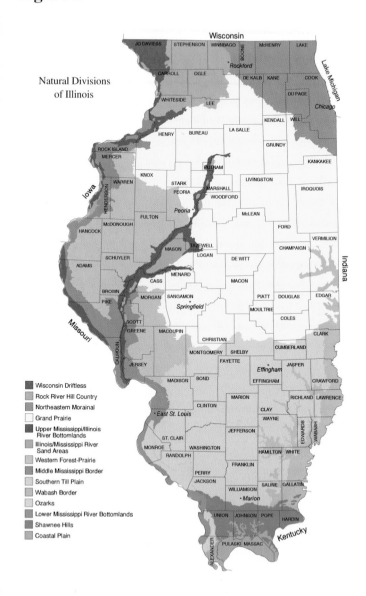

Natural Divisions of Illinois

Wisconsin Driftless
Rock River Hill Country
Northeastern Moraional
Grand Prairie
Upper Mississippi/Illinois River Bottomlands
Illinois/Mississippi River Sand Areas
Western Forest-Prairie
Middle Mississippi Border
Southern Till Plain
Wabash Border
Ozarks
Lower Mississippi River Bottomlands
Shawnee Hills
Coastal Plain

and brought them under cultivation. Thus, an entire ecosystem was nearly eliminated, as were some amphibians and reptiles adapted to it. During the past 100 years, urban development, road construction, forest fragmentation, siltation and chemical pollution of streams, containment of major rivers within levees, and drainage of wetlands have further altered and fragmented ranges of amphibians and reptiles.

Conservation

Endangered and Threatened Species

In 1972, the Illinois legislature passed the Illinois Endangered Species Protection Act to control exploitation of animals and plants and prevent their continued loss. The act has been revised several times. Under provisions of the act, permits are required to possess, take, transport, sell, offer for sale, give, or otherwise dispose of individuals of any species protected by either the Illinois or the federal endangered species act. By definition, a State Endangered Species is any species that is in danger of extinction as a breeding species in Illinois. A State Threatened Species is any breeding species that is likely to become a state endangered species within the foreseeable future in Illinois. Decisions to list are made by the Illinois Endangered Species Protection Board (appointed by the governor) with advice from Endangered Species Technical Advisory committees composed of experts from around the state. Seven amphibians and fifteen reptiles currently are state-listed. They are listed here as they appear in the *Checklist of Endangered and Threatened Animals and Plants of Illinois*, produced by the Illinois Endangered Species Protection Board.

Common Name	Species	Status
Silvery salamander	*Ambystoma platineum*	Endangered
Hellbender	*Cryptobranchus alleganiensis*	Endangered
Dusky salamander	*Desmognathus fuscus*	Endangered
Jefferson salamander	*Ambystoma jeffersonianum*	Threatened

Four-toed salamander	*Hemidactylium scutatum*	Threatened
Bird-voiced treefrog	*Hyla avivoca*	Threatened
Illinois chorus frog	*Pseudacris streckeri*	Threatened
Alligator snapping turtle	*Macroclemys temminckii*	Endangered
Spotted turtle	*Clemmys guttata*	Endangered
River cooter	*Pseudemys concinna*	Endangered
Illinois mud turtle	*Kinosternon flavescens*	Endangered
Blanding's turtle	*Emydoidea blandingii*	Threatened
Coachwhip	*Masticophis flagellum*	Endangered
Broad-banded water snake	*Nerodia fasciata*	Endangered
Eastern massasauga	*Sistrurus catenatus*	Endangered
Eastern ribbon snake	*Thamnophis sauritus*	Endangered
Kirtland's snake	*Clonophis kirtlandii*	Threatened
Great Plains rat snake	*Elaphe guttata emoryi*	Threatened
Western hognose snake	*Heterodon nasicus*	Threatened
Mississippi green water snake	*Nerodia cyclopion*	Threatened
Flathead snake	*Tantilla gracilis*	Threatened
Timber rattlesnake	*Crotalus horridus*	Threatened

Collecting, Keeping, and Permits

Keeping and caring for captive amphibians and reptiles can be an emotionally satisfying and educationally enriching hobby, and recently their popularity as pets has been growing tremendously. Quite naturally, concerns about protecting landowners and depleting natural populations have led to some legal restrictions. For example, the state considers venomous reptiles and "life-threatening" reptiles (crocodilians and large constricting snakes) to be dangerous. It is illegal to keep them, and licensed pet stores may not sell any boa or python over six feet long. Because of concerns about infections of salmonella, it is illegal to sell within the United States any turtle with a carapace length under four inches. Many cities have ordinances that ban as pets venomous lizards and snakes as well as large nonvenomous lizards and snakes. You should consult the Illinois Department of Natural Resources and municipal Animal Control Officers for details.

Illinois State law prohibits the use of any wild-caught amphibian or reptile, or any of their parts, eggs, or offspring, for commercial purposes. For personal enjoyment, a person may collect nonlisted Illinois species but none may be sold or traded.

They may be captured by any device that is not designed to cause death or serious injury. If released, individuals must be returned to the place where they were captured. Check with the Illinois Department of Natural Resources, Office of Law Enforcement, for details on the capture limits and season. Offspring produced in captivity are exempt from the possession limit for 90 days, but they may not be sold, bought, or traded.

With a valid fishing license one may take turtles (by hand, hook and line, or dip net) and bullfrogs (by hand, hook and line, dip net, gig, pitchfork, spear, or bow and arrow) within designated daily catch and possession limits.

It is illegal to collect within Shawnee National Forest, National Wildlife Refuges, nature preserves, county forest preserves, and all Department of Natural Resources owned or managed areas (state parks, fish and wildlife areas, natural areas, conservation areas, etc.) without appropriate permits. Permission must also be secured from all private landowners.

Because of their limited or historically greatly reduced populations in Illinois, state endangered and threatened species (see list, pp. 7–8), even those not collected in the state, may not be possessed, harbored, cared for, sold, offered for sale, handled, harassed, harmed, or imported without a permit from the Illinois Department of Natural Resources.

Presently, no Illinois amphibian or reptile is listed as federally threatened or endangered but, through a memorandum of understanding between the Illinois Department of Natural Resources and the U.S. Fish and Wildlife Service, the copperbelly water snake is protected as though it were listed.

Habitat Improvement for Amphibians and Reptiles

Human activities have profoundly affected the distribution and abundance of amphibians and reptiles in Illinois. As the state's natural landscape has been transformed over the past 150 years, natural habitats have been modified and converted to meet human needs, being fragmented by railroads, highways, deforestation, prairie agriculture, and drainage of great expanses of marsh and floodplain swamps. Although the state still has large areas of surface water, it is largely in man-made lakes constructed at the expense of stream habitat. All of these impoundments, and most smaller farm ponds, are stocked with fish that prey on amphibians and reptiles and, in some cases, eliminate them. Channelization of other streams has eliminated large areas of floodplain and slough habitats. Faced with such widespread habitat loss, which shows no signs of slowing, amphibians and reptiles can benefit greatly from even modest forms of habitat improvement.

Making habitats more suitable for amphibians and reptiles often is simple if you concentrate on the ecological requirements of particular species: food, shelter, basking sites (for reptiles), egg-deposition sites, larval habitat (for most amphibians), and hibernating sites. Two simple modifications that will benefit most amphibians and many reptiles are (1) excavate small seasonal pools that may dry up in late summer or fish-free permanent ponds in or near woods or fallow fields, and (2) allow emergent and shoreline vegetation to develop naturally. In addition to providing egg-laying sites and habitat for the aquatic larval stages of amphibians, ponds will increase populations of many of the invertebrates fed upon by amphibians, many of which, in turn, are eaten by reptiles. Over the years, many seasonal pools, water-filled tire ruts, and poorly drained lands have been drained, developed, or poisoned for mosquito control. Unfortunately, many species of amphibians and reptiles cannot survive without these aquatic habitats. Managing a pond for amphibians and reptiles is largely a matter of letting nature take its course, and keeping fish and livestock away from it. Logs, rocks, and brush piles along the shores will provide shelter and basking sites.

Reptiles must have access to suitable basking places so they can regulate their body temperature. Good basking places not only allow exposure to direct sunlight but also provide crevices into which individuals can retreat once heated or when threatened by a predator. Brush and rock piles along edges of woodlands, fields, ditches, and streams can meet these needs and encourage populations of prey organisms (invertebrates and small rodents) as well. The key to managing a woodland for amphibians and reptiles is habitat diversity. Dead standing and fallen trees, logs, bark, and small brush piles offer shelter, dens, and places where lizard and snake eggs may be laid as well as increase the availability of food organisms.

Highways as Habitat for Herps

Tremendous numbers of amphibians and reptiles perish annually because of a deadly, relatively new predator for which they have no adaptive defense, one that kills but does not eat—the motor vehicle. Heavy-bodied animals like turtles and large snakes are easily recognized by passing motorists, but lizards, small snakes, frogs, and salamanders flattened into the pavement usually are not. In some places, especially during warm summer rains and during the autumn, the carnage is much greater than most would imagine. During five autumn days in 1991, 150 brown snakes, most of them killed by vehicles, were found on 1.3 miles of secondary hard-surfaced road. Illinois is crisscrossed by gravel roads and hard-surfaced highways. It is estimated that there are over 138,000 miles of roads in Illinois, and it is difficult in much of the state to stray more than a short distance from a road. Amphibians and reptiles cross roads when moving among overwintering sites, summer feeding grounds, nesting sites, or bodies of water where eggs and tadpoles develop. Besides forming barriers to movement among these habitat components, highways warmed by the sun can be fatally seductive to snakes using them to raise their body temperatures after a cool night, or to a frog drawn to insects attracted by automobile or street lights. Closing all highways to protect amphibians and reptiles from this new source of mortality is not practical, but there is no justification for running over them on purpose. At least one gravel road in Shawnee National Forest is closed biannually so amphibians and reptiles can migrate safely between their rocky overwintering sites and summer habitat, and at least one project is attempting to get a state-threatened snake to migrate in tunnels under a road rather than over it. Roads are not entirely harmful to amphibians and reptiles. Many of them are raised above a coarse rocky base that provides underground cavities for shelter and overwintering for some species, and water-filled ditches alongside are excellent summer habitat for many species.

Declining Amphibian Populations

Over the last few years there has been increased concern about worldwide declines and even extinctions of frog and toad species. Habitat destruction and degradation are clearly responsible in most cases but alarming declines have occurred in relatively pristine environments such as the rainforests of eastern Australia and the cloud forests of Costa Rica. Closer to Illinois, biologists in the upper Midwest have been noticing the disappearance of our smallest frog, the cricket frog (*Acris crepitans*). Until the early 1980s, cricket frogs were among the most common anurans in Illinois, and they could be found in almost every county. Today, only a handful of populations are known from the northern one-third of Illinois. The puzzling part of this observation is that cricket frogs do not appear to be declining in the southern two-thirds of the state. Among the causes that have been suggested for this mysterious observation are buildup of toxic substances (pesticides, heavy metals) in the frogs' breeding ponds, habitat fragmentation, increased parasite levels, and increased levels of ultraviolet radiation.

The Declining Amphibian Population Task Force (DAPTF) is a global network of biologists and conservationists concerned with the issue of declining amphibian populations. The DAPTF has two primary objectives: (1) to determine the geography and extent of declines and disappearances of amphibians, and (2) to determine the causes of amphibian declines and disappearances. The DAPTF operates through a network of working groups, over 80 of which represent different regions of the world, that collect geographical data on amphibian declines and their causes. Other issue-based working groups are concerned with specific topics, including disease and pathology, monitoring techniques, chemical contaminants, and climatic and atmospheric change. The United States Central Division Working Group includes the states of Iowa, Missouri, Illinois, Indiana, and Ohio.

How to Use This Book

This guide is intended to aid biologists, naturalists, teachers, land managers, law enforcement officials, and students in the identification of amphibians and reptiles found in Illinois. It is meant to be used in the field, so the characters stressed in the keys and species accounts can be viewed with the unaided eye or, at most, a small hand lens. Occasionally, technical terms are used to describe anatomical features; these terms are defined in the Glossary.

The species are grouped according to systematic relationships: salamanders, frogs, turtles, lizards, and snakes. This means that similar-looking species are usually, but not always, grouped together. The book is set up so that identification can be achieved either by using the traditional dichotomous keys on pages 20–54 or by using the color photographs and "key characters" section included in each species account. The dichotomous keys are the most effective way to identify an animal, but some readers unfamiliar with keys may find the photographs a more user-friendly starting point. Only a handful of the 102 species covered by this guide are distributed statewide; therefore, many species may be eliminated from consideration because they do not occur in the geographic region you are studying.

Explanation of Species Accounts

Each species account has three components: text, photograph, and range map.

Text
Each account lists the common and scientific names of the species. The taxonomic arrangement and names used in this guide follow the expanded third edition of *A Field Guide to the*

Reptiles and Amphibians of Eastern and Central North America (Conant & Collins 1998). Exceptions to this are: *Rana sphenocephala* is recognized by the International Commission on Zoological Nomenclature as the appropriate name for the southern leopard frog instead of *Rana utricularia*; Fowler's toad is treated as a full species, *Bufo fowleri*; the upland chorus frog is treated as a full species, *Pseudacris feriarum*; the Mississippi map turtle, *Graptemys kohnii*, is not recognized as a distinct species; the Ouachita map turtle, *Graptemys ouachitensis*, is treated as a species distinct from *G. pseudogeographica*; and the western worm snake is treated as a subspecies, *Carphophis amoenus vermis*. Each species account contains the following text components: key characters, similar species, subspecies, description, habitat, natural history, and status.

Key characters. This section lists the most useful and prominent features for identification of each species.

Similar species. Many species of amphibians and reptiles are similar in appearance. This section lists one or more species that often are confused with the focal species.

Subspecies. The subspecies designation is used to describe geographic variation in a species. Subspecies are geographically separated throughout most of the species range, but may mix in a narrow zone where they meet. This is known as a zone of intergradation and the individuals in this zone are referred to as intergrades. If subspecies have been described for a species, those known to occur in Illinois are listed in this section.

Description. A more thorough list of characters than those appearing in the Key Characters section is given. Average or maximum size is also given.

Habitat. Amphibian and reptile species display a wide range of habitat preferences. A few are found throughout the state, but most are restricted to a smaller area by such factors as climate, dominant vegetation, and prey items. This section describes the specific habitat attributes for each species.

Natural History. This section lists the activity period, diet, predators, reproductive data, and any unique behaviors for each species.

Status. This section gives information on distribution and abundance in Illinois. If a species has state or federal listing status (endangered or threatened), that is indicated.

Photographs
In most cases, the photographs used in this guide are of Illinois specimens. Exceptions were made for species that are difficult to obtain in Illinois because of rarity. In these cases, specimens from other states were used. The photos are not to scale, so the reader should refer to the text section of the species account for information on size. Inset photos have been provided for some species to show details of diagnostic characters and illustrate differences between adults and juveniles or subspecies. Most of the photographs in this guide were taken by Michael Redmer (MR), free-lance photographer and biologist. Other photos were taken by Scott Ballard (SB), a District Heritage Biologist with the Illinois Department of Natural Resources in Marion; Eric Routman (ER), Assistant Professor in the Department of Biological Sciences at San Francisco State University; R. Wayne Van Devender (RWV), Professor of Biology at Appalachian State University in Boone, North Carolina; and the authors (RAB, EOM, & CAP). Credits are given in the legend of each photo.

Range Maps
The maps show the counties for which a vouchered specimen, photo, or sight record of the focal species exists. The information used to prepare the maps was taken from lists of cataloged specimens or photographs provided by the following collections: Academy of Natural Sciences, Philadelphia; American Museum of Natural History, New York; Auburn University Museum, Auburn, AL; Bobby Witcher Memorial Collection, University of Missouri, Columbia; Burpee Museum of Natural History, Rockford, IL; California Academy of Sciences, San Francisco; Carnegie Museum of Natural History, Pittsburgh; Chicago Academy of Science; Field Museum of Natural History, Chicago; Florida Museum of Natural History, University of Florida, Gainesville; Harlan D. Walley Collection, De Kalb, IL; Illinois

Gainesville; Harlan D. Walley Collection, De Kalb, IL; Illinois Natural History Survey, Champaign; Illinois State Museum, Springfield; Louisiana State University Museum of Natural Science, Baton Rouge; Milwaukee Public Museum; Museum of Comparative Zoology, Harvard University, Cambridge, MA; Museum of Vertebrate Zoology, University of California, Berkeley; National Museum of Natural History, Smithsonian Institution, Washington, DC; Natural History Museum of Los Angeles County; Nebraska State Museum, University of Nebraska, Lincoln; Principia College, Elsah, IL; Minton Herpetological Collection, Indianapolis; Southern Illinois University at Carbondale; Southern Illinois University at Edwardsville; Texas Cooperative Wildlife Collection, Texas A&M University, College Station; Tulane University Museum of Natural History, New Orleans; University of Illinois Museum of Natural History, Champaign; University of Kansas, Museum of Natural History, Lawrence; University of Michigan Museum of Zoology, Ann Arbor; and University of Wisconsin-Stevens Point. Only a fraction of the nearly 28,000 Illinois specimens listed by these collections has been examined by the authors, so these records must be considered tentative. Sight records were taken from the literature, reliable biologists and naturalists, and the Illinois Department of Natural Resources Natural Heritage Database (NHD).

In the range maps, hatching indicates a record is based on data prior to the arbitrary cutoff of 1980; solid indicates post-1980. However, if more than one category of record exists for a species-county combination, the order of precedence is vouchered, photo, then sight—regardless of the date of the records. This means that a pre-1980 vouchered record takes precedence over a post-1980 photo or sight record. This is potentially misleading because readers may conclude that species have declined in counties where there are no post-1980 records. In some cases declines surely have occurred, but in others the absence of post-1980 records reflects the lack of recent field work in the area or the fact that the species is so common that no one bothered to collect more recent specimens. This problem is not restricted to range maps with a temporal aspect. Keep in mind that all range maps based on data culled from natural history collections or literature records can misrepresent species distributions because it is unlikely that all areas of a given region have been visited with equal frequency. We know, for example, that collection efforts are often greater around large cities, universities, or outstanding natural features. Therefore, it is best to view these maps as rough guides to known locations and avoid inferences about exact distribution or temporal changes in distribution. These maps can also be used to guide future collection efforts to those areas and species currently underrepresented in collections and the literature.

Range maps for several species require additional explanation because of taxonomic confusion. For example, until the 1970s the plains and southern leopard frogs were not recognized as species distinct from the northern leopard frog. Therefore, many cataloged specimens and much of the early literature on the northern leopard frog may actually refer to one or a combination of these species; thus, the range maps of the leopard frogs show only those records that have been explicitly assigned to one of the three species. In most cases the authors or other reliable authorities have examined the specimens. The second problematic group consists of the western and upland chorus frogs, which were considered a single species until recently. Our maps use an arbitrary geographical cutoff to distinguish among these species' records. In reality the two species' ranges overlap in southern Illinois. The third problematic group is the gray treefrog complex. Individuals of these two species are distinguishable only by chromosome number, cell size, or mating call. Our range map makes no attempt to distinguish between the two. The final group consists of the false and Ouachita map turtles, which were recognized as distinct species in the 1990s. Our range maps show only those records that have been explicitly assigned to each of the species. Again, the authors or reliable authorities have examined the specimens. Much work remains concerning the distribution of these four groups.

Glossary of Terms

Adpressed limbs – front leg extended backward and the back leg forward in an attempt to overlap the limbs (Fig. 5)

Amplexus – embrace used by amphibians during mating; initiated by the male.

Anal plate – scale(s) that covers the vent (Fig. 27)

Balancer – slender projection on each side of the head of recently hatched salamander larvae

Biphasic – having two distinct parts

Bridge – bony connection between the upper and lower shells of a turtle (Fig. 15)

Carapace – upper shell of a turtle (Fig. 13a)

Cirrus (pl. **cirri**) – downward projection of the upper lip, below the nostril

Cloaca – internal chamber at the base of the tail that receives the digestive, urinary, and reproductive tracts

Costal grooves – vertical grooves on the side of the body each corresponding to the location of a rib (Fig. 2)

Dorsal – upper surface or back

Dorsolateral fold – ridge or fold of skin along the side of the back of frogs (Fig. 9)

Eft – terrestrial stage in newt's life cycle between metamorphosis and first return to breeding pond as aquatic adult

Femoral – referring to the thigh region

Fossorial – living mainly underground, burrowing

Gill filament – smallest (secondary) branch of the external gill (Fig. 3)

Gill ramus (pl. **rami**) – stouter, central (primary) branch of the external gill; the filaments project from the rami (Fig. 3).

Gill slit – the slit or hole through which water passes from the throat to the exterior (Fig. 3)

Gravid – full of eggs

Groin – where the thigh attaches to the body on the belly

Gular fold – a fold of skin across the throat (Fig. 3)

Hedonic – pertaining to stimulation during courtship

Hemipenis – one of the paired, protrusible, copulatory organs of male lizards and snakes

Intergradation – interbreeding among members of two or more subspecies along a zone of contact

Keratinized – covered with a hard, horny substance (keratin) similar to fingernails

Larva (pl. **larvae**) – the immature form; in amphibians, aquatic with fins and gills

Maxillary – pertaining to the upper jaw

Mental – on the underside of the chin

Metamorphosis – the change or transformation from larva to juvenile

Nasolabial groove – slit or furrow from the nostril opening to the upper lip (Fig. 4)

Operculum – flap of skin covering the gill slit

Oviduct – tube that carries eggs to the cloaca

Parotoid gland – poison-producing gland on the top of a toad's head, usually behind the eye

Plastron – bottom part of a turtle's shell (Fig. 13b)

Polyploid – having more than the usual two sets of chromosomes

Riparian – found along rivers and streams

Scute – large scale, especially in turtles (Fig. 16)

Snout-vent length – distance between the tip of the snout and the posterior end of the vent

Spermatophore – structure produced by most male salamanders that includes a gelatinous stalk with a packet of sperm on top

Tibial – referring to the lower leg or tibia (Fig. 9)

Tympanum – rounded, external eardrum on the side of the head (Fig. 9)

Tympanic fold – fold of skin around the eardrum

Vent – external opening of the cloaca

Ventral – underside or belly

Vernal – pertaining to the spring season

Vomeronasal organ – organ located in the roof of the mouth of a snake and used for smelling or tasting particles picked up from the air by the tongue

Yolk sac – small external sac of nutrients carried by hatchlings

Key to Amphibians and Reptiles of Illinois

ADULT AND LARVAL SALAMANDER KEY

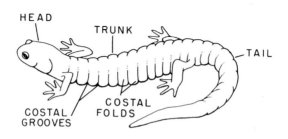

Figure 2. Salamander external anatomy.

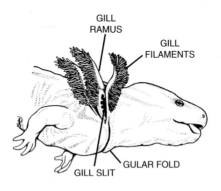

Figure 3. External gills of larval salamander.

1a. External gills absent..2

1b. External gills present (Fig. 3)..19

2a. Gill slits (Fig. 3) 1 pair; eyelids absent [body wrinkled and
      flattened, with a fold of skin along each side; a flap of skin
      on the trailing edge of each leg]............................ Hellbender

2b. Gill slits (Fig. 3) absent; eyelids present................................3

3a. Nasolabial grooves (Fig. 4) present......................................4

3b. Nasolabial grooves (Fig. 4) absent.......................................11

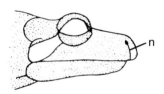

Figure 4. Head of salamander showing nasolabial groove (n).

4a. Hind foot with 4 toes; base of tail constricted; belly white
      with black spots....................................Four-toed Salamander

4b. Hind foot with 5 toes; base of tail not constricted; belly not
      white with black spots..5

5a. Light line from eye to angle of jaw............Dusky Salamander

5b. Light line from eye to angle of jaw absent.............................6

6a. Groundcolor of body yellow, tan, orange, or red; belly white, orange, or yellow 7

6b. Groundcolor of back and belly dark gray, brown or black....9

7a. Costal folds 3 or more between adpressed limbs (Fig. 5); back with pair of dark brown stripes.......................................
....Southern Two-lined Salamander

7b. Costal folds 2 or fewer between adpressed limbs (Fig. 5); back without brown stripes...8

Figure 5. Lateral view of adult salamander showing three costal folds between adpressed limbs.

8a. Groundcolor of body orange or red; back with scattered black spots; sides of tail with scattered black spots.................
....Cave Salamander

8b. Groundcolor of body yellow or orange-yellow; back with clustered black spots; sides of tail uniformly dark or with dark vertical zigzag bars........................Longtail Salamander

9a. Back black with small white spots..............Slimy Salamander

9b. Back dark gray with fine white stippling or with a yellow to red midback stripe...10

10a. Tail usually longer than snout-vent length; midback stripe, if present, always straight-edged; upper front legs without orange or red pigment..........................Redback Salamander

10b. Tail usually shorter than snout-vent length; midback stripe, if present, straight-edged or zigzag; upper front legs with orange or red pigment..............................Zigzag Salamander

11a. Costal grooves absent; gular fold (Fig. 3) absent....................
....Eastern Newt

11b. Costal grooves present; gular fold (Fig. 3) present.................
....12

12a. Back dark with white or silvery crossbands...........................
....Marbled Salamander

12b. Back dark, but without white or silvery crossbands.............13

13a. Back with yellow or orange spots......................................14

13b. Back without yellow or orange spots.................................15

14a. Back with circular yellow spots of nearly equal size and in 2 rows; belly uniformly dark gray..............Spotted Salamander

14b. Back with irregular yellow spots of unequal size, and not organized into rows; belly usually marked with yellow spots...Tiger Salamander

15a. Costal grooves (Fig. 2) 10–11; body short and stocky; head
width 23% or more of snout-vent length....Mole Salamander

15b. Costal grooves (Fig. 2) 12 or more; body not short and
stocky; head width less than 23% of snout-vent length......16

16a. Neck wider than head; snout very short; lower jaw projecting slightly beyond upper jaw (Fig. 6a).................................
....Smallmouth Salamander

16b. Head wider than neck; snout long and broad; lower jaw not
projecting beyond upper jaw (Fig. 6b) 17

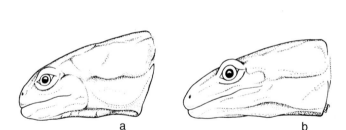

Figure 6. Side view of head of adult salamanders: (a) protruding lower
jaw in the smallmouth salamander, (b) even lower jaw in the Jefferson
salamander.

17a. All or nearly all individuals female; known from one
location in Vermilion County.................Silvery Salamander

17b. Males and females present; not known from Vermilion
County...18

18a. Groundcolor black or nearly so; back and sides heavily marked with small bluish spots, vent surrounded by black...Blue-spotted Salamander

18b. Groundcolor dark brown to lead gray, back and sides only lightly marked with bluish flecks (usually concentrated along lower sides); vent usually surrounded by gray.............. ....Jefferson Salamander

19a. Gill slits (Fig. 3) absent.......................neotenic Eastern Newt

19b. Gill slits (Fig. 3) present...20

20a. Hind legs absent[1]; body eel-like; costal grooves (Fig. 2) 30 or more..Lesser Siren

20b. Hind legs present; body not eel-like; costal grooves (Fig. 2) fewer than 30...21

21a. Upper fin low and limited to the tail (Fig. 7a)....................22

21b. Upper fin high and extending well on to the trunk anterior to the vent (Fig. 7b)..26

---

[1]Because larval legs develop gradually after hatching, number of legs is not a useful trait for identifying larvae under about 25 mm total length.

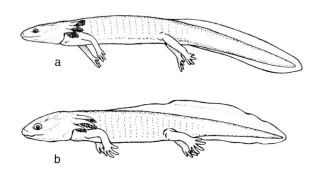

Figure 7. Side view of larval salamanders: (a) upper fin low and limited to tail, gill ramus shorter than filaments; (b) upper fin high and extending well anterior to the vent, gill ramus much longer than filaments.

22a. Midback stripe always present, dark, and bordered on each side by a light stripe; open gill slits (Fig. 3) 2...... Mudpuppy

22b. Midback stripe, if present, light and not bordered by a light stripe; open gill slits (Fig. 3) 3 or 4.....................................23

23a. Gill slits (Fig. 3) 4; gill rami shorter than gill filaments (Fig. 7a); gills glistening white........................Dusky Salamander

23b. Gill slits (Fig. 3) 3; gill rami much longer than filaments (Fig. 7b); gills pigmented..24

24a. Throat darkly pigmented on anterior half only (Fig. 8a); body pigment encroaching onto the belly beyond bases of limbs; bottoms of hind feet pigmented......Cave Salamander

24b. Throat not or only sparsely pigmented on anterior half (Fig. 8b); body pigment not encroaching onto belly beyond bases of limbs; bottoms of hind feet not pigmented...........25

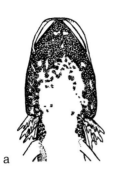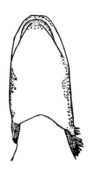

a   b

Figure 8. Throats of larval salamanders: (a) throat darkly pigmented on anterior half, (b) throat not, or only sparsely, pigmented on anterior half.

25a. Back marked with a series of paired light spots, which may fuse with a midback light stripe; throat pigment absent........ ....Southern Two-lined Salamander

25b. Back marked with a light stripe, never paired light spots; throat pigment usually sparse and restricted to the anterior third (Fig. 8b)...Longtail Salamander

26a. Gill slits (Fig. 3) in 3 pairs; never more than 4 toes on hind feet[2]...Four-toed Salamander

26b. Gill slits (Fig. 3) in 4 pairs; 5 toes on hind feet...................27

27a. Costal grooves (Fig. 2) absent; side of the head with dark stripe that continues through eye......................Eastern Newt

27b. Costal grooves (Fig. 2) present; side of the head without dark stripe that continues through eye 28

---

[2]Number of toes is not a reliable trait for distinguishing small four-toed salamander larvae from small larval *Ambystoma* that are still developing toes.

28a. Throat well pigmented (Fig. 8a)............................29

28b. Throat without pigment or with pigment bordering jaws
     only (Fig. 8b)...31

29a. Back of small larvae without dark, transverse bands; sides
     of body with light spots; belly uniformly covered with
     small dots of pigment............................Marbled Salamander

29b. Back of small larvae with dark, transverse bands; sides of
     body without light spots; belly not uniformly covered with
     small dots of pigment...30

30a. Costal grooves (Fig. 2) 14–16; belly unpigmented, or with
     a narrow midline of pigment; side of head of small larvae
     without dark stripes........................Smallmouth Salamander

30b. Costal grooves (Fig. 2) 10–11; belly with dark, central
     stripe bordered by light stripes; side of head of small larvae
     with 1 or 2 dark stripes..............................Mole Salamander

31a. Toes flattened, broad at base and pointed at tip.....................
     ....Tiger Salamander

31b. Toes not flattened, broad at base, or pointed at tip............32

32a. Head conspicuously large and much wider than the trunk;
     tail fin intensely pigmented and mottled with black; back of
     small larvae with dark transverse bands ....
     ....Jefferson, Blue-spotted, or Silvery Salamander

32b. Head not notably large nor much wider than the trunk; tail
     fin not intensely pigmented or distinctly mottled; back of
     small larvae without dark transverse bands...........................
     ....Spotted Salamander

ADULT FROG AND TOAD KEY

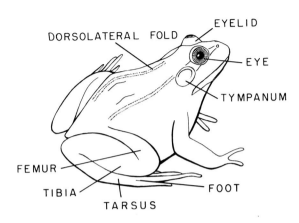

Figure 9. Frog external anatomy.

1a. Heel of each hind foot with 1 or 2 horny spades (Fig. 10).....2

1b. Horny spades absent from hind feet....................................4

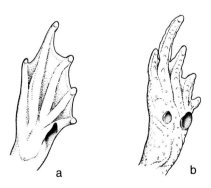

Figure 10. Hind feet of toads: (a) single horny spade on spadefoot, (b) 2 horny spades on true toads.

2a. Heel of each hind foot with 1 horny spade (Fig. 10a); parotoid glands (Fig. 11) round and small; pupils of eyes vertical..Eastern Spadefoot Toad

2b. Heel of each hind foot with 1 large and 1 small spade (Fig. 10b); parotoid glands (Fig. 11) oval and large; pupils of eyes horizontal or round [numerous warts on body].....................3

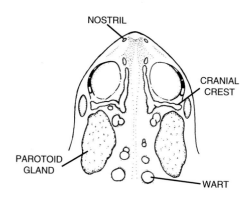

Figure 11. Dorsal aspect of head of toad showing features useful in identification.

3a. Back with small spots that typically include 1 or 2 warts; belly usually profusely mottled with black; tibial warts distinctly larger than femoral warts.................American Toad

3b. Back with large spots that include 3 or more warts; belly pigment confined to a small spot on the chest; tibial warts not distinctly larger than femoral warts.............Fowler's Toad

4a. Fold of skin behind head; head less than one-fourth snout-vent length; tympanum absent.....Eastern Narrowmouth Toad

4b. No fold of skin behind head; head approximately one-third of snout-vent length; tympanum present...............................5

5a. Tips of toes expanded to form disc-like toe pads...................6

5b. Tips of toes not expanded to form disc-like toe pads...........13

6a. Toe pads small and inconspicuous, not wider than end of toe; snout-vent length less than 35 mm.......................................7

6b. Toe pads conspicuous, wider than end of toe; maximum snout-vent length 50 mm...10

7a. Toes fully webbed; back with numerous small warts; marking between eyes dark and triangle-shaped.....................
....Cricket Frog

7b. Toes not webbed or webbing restricted to a small flap of skin on each side of digit; back without warts; marking between eyes absent...8

8a. Body short and stout; lateral dark stripe passing through each eye and onto shoulder; a dark spot beneath each eye; front legs large and muscular......................Strecker's Chorus Frog

8b. Body flattened and elongate; lateral stripe passing through eye reaches beyond shoulder; no dark spot beneath eye; front legs not large and muscular...9

9a. Back with 3 distinct longitudinal stripes, each stripe as wide as the space between the stripes.............Western Chorus Frog

9b. Back without broken longitudinal stripes or, if present, stripes one-half as wide as the space between them................
....Upland Chorus Frog

10a. Groundcolor of back tan or pink, back with distinct dark X-mark..Spring Peeper

10b. Groundcolor of back dark; back without X-mark...............11

11a. Back green and without a star-shaped blotch; light spot under eye absent...Green Treefrog

11b. Back variable in color, usually with a star-shaped blotch; light spot present under eye...12

12a. Underside of thighs bright orange or yellow; snout-vent length to 60 mm...Gray Treefrog

12b. Underside of thighs not bright orange or yellow; snout-vent length under 50 m.................................Bird-voiced Treefrog

13a. Dorsolateral folds (Fig. 9) absent; tympanic fold well developed..Bullfrog

13b. Pair of dorsolateral folds (Fig. 9) extending onto back; tympanic fold inconspicuous...14

14a. Dorsolateral folds (Fig. 9) terminating just beyond midback ....Green Frog

14b. Dorsolateral folds (Fig. 9) extending length of back..........15

15a. Dark mask passing through eye and tympanum; back without distinct spots, but may have dashes.........Wood Frog

15b. No dark mask passing through eye and tympanum; back with distinct spots..16

16a. Jaws mottled; dorsal spots closely crowded together in a reticulated pattern...Crawfish Frog

16b. Jaws not mottled; dorsal spots not closely crowded...........17

17a. Dorsal spots square or rectangular and regularly arranged in 2 rows between the dorsolateral folds (Fig. 12a); concealed surfaces of thighs yellow...................................Pickerel Frog

17b. Dorsal spots irregular in shape and arrangement; concealed surfaces of thighs white..18

18a. Dorsolateral folds wide and moderately raised; dorsal spots larger than eye and ringed in white or cream (Fig. 12b); snout usually with dark spot..............Northern Leopard Frog

18b. Dorsolateral folds narrow and distinctly raised; dorsal spots average smaller than eye and not ringed in white; snout with or without spot..19

19a. Dorsolateral folds broken near groin and displaced toward midline (Fig. 12c); snout rounded, usually with a spot........... ....Plains Leopard Frog

19b. Dorsolateral folds usually continuous, but if broken, broken sections never displaced toward midline (Fig. 12d); snout pointed, usually without a spot..........Southern Leopard Frog

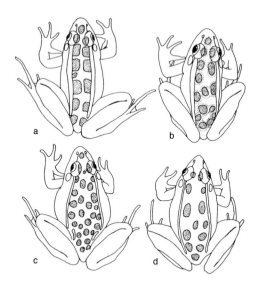

Figure 12. Dorsal patterns: (a) pickerel frog, (b) northern leopard frog, (c) plains leopard frog, (d) southern leopard frog.

ADULT TURTLE KEY

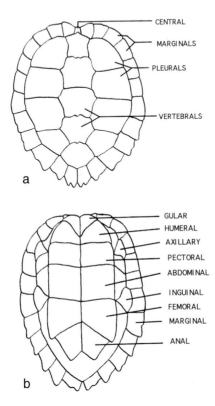

Figure 13. Carapace (a) and plastron (b) of false map turtle.

1a. Bony shell covered with leathery skin.....................................2

1b. Bony shell covered with large scutes (Fig. 13a)....................3

2a. Anterior edge of carapace with small tubercles or spines; interior of nostrils with horizontal projections (Fig. 14a)........ ....Spiny Softshell

2b. Anterior edge of carapace smooth; interior of nostrils lack projections (Fig. 14b)....................................Smooth Softshell

3a. Plastron with 11 or more plates contacting at midline (Fig. 13b); tail short (< half shell length)..............................4

3b. Plastron with fewer than 11 plates contacting at midline (Fig. 15); tail long (> half shell length) 5

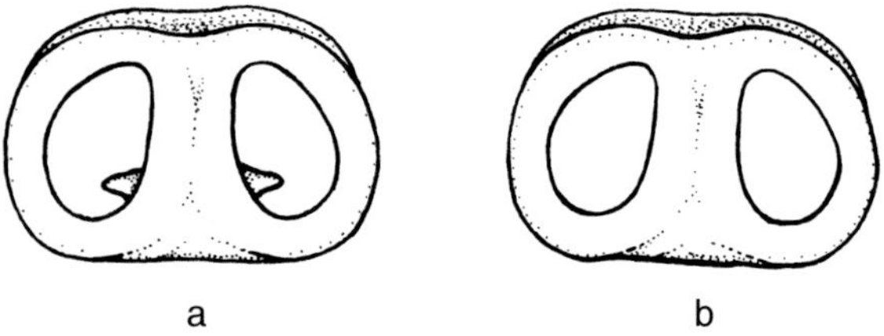

a   b

Figure 14. Looking head-on into the nostrils of softshell turtles: (a) spiny softshell showing horizontal projections, (b) smooth softshell showing rounded nostrils.

4a. Carapace (usually) with 11 pairs of marginal scutes (Fig. 17); plastron with < 6 pairs of scutes (Fig. 17)......................6

4b. Carapace (usually) with 12 pairs of marginal scutes (Fig. 13a); plastron with 6 pairs of scutes (Fig. 13b)......................8

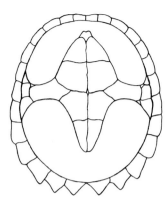

Figure 15. Plastron of snapping turtle showing 9 plastral plates. The horizontal elements are part of the bridge and not considered plastral plates.

5a. Carapace with single row of marginal scutes and 3 low keels that disappear with age....................................Snapping Turtle

5b. Carapace with an extra row of scutes between marginals and pleural scutes 1–3 on each side (Fig. 16) and 3 prominent keels that do not disappear with age ....
....Alligator Snapping Turtle

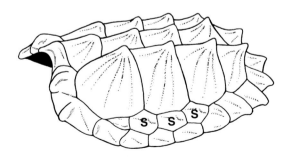

Figure 16. Side view of carapace of alligator snapping turtle showing extra row of scutes called supramarginals (S) between marginals and pleural scutes 1–3.

6a. Skin showing between plastral scutes; pectoral scutes square (Fig. 17a); a single poorly developed plastral hinge anteriorly ....Common Musk Turtle

6b. Skin not showing between plastral scutes; pectoral scutes triangular (Fig. 17b); 2 well-developed plastral hinges.........7

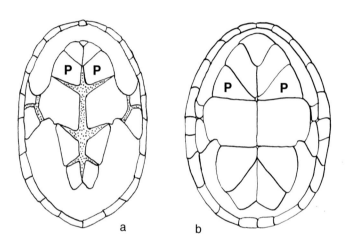

Figure 17. Plastrons: (a) common musk turtle with skin between plastral scutes (stippled areas) and squarish pectoral scutes (P); (b) yellow mud turtle without skin between plastral scutes and triangular pectoral scutes (P).

7a. Marginals 8 and 9 of approximately equal height (Fig. 18a)... ....Eastern Mud Turtle

7b. Marginal 9 much higher than 8 (Fig. 18b)............................... ....Yellow Mud Turtle

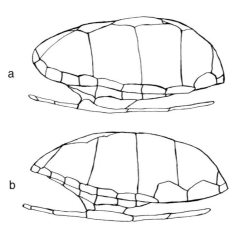

Figure 18. Side view of carapace: (a) eastern mud turtle showing marginals 8 and 9 of approximately equal height; (b) yellow mud turtle showing marginal 9 much higher than 8.

8a. Plastron hinged between pectoral and abdominal scutes.......9

8b. Plastron not hinged...11

9a. Chin and throat bright yellow; upper jaw notched...................
....Blanding's Turtle

9b. Chin and throat not bright yellow; upper jaw hooked..........10

10a. Carapace and plastron with radiating yellow lines; peak of carapace flattened and lacking a keel.........Ornate Box Turtle

10b. Carapace pattern variable; plastron lacking discreet pattern of light lines; peak of carapace dome-like with median keel...Eastern Box Turtle

11a. Carapace black with prominent yellow spots...Spotted Turtle

11b. Carapace variable without prominent yellow spots...............
....12

12a. Marginal scutes or plastron marked with red...Painted Turtle

12b. Marginal scutes and plastron not marked with red.............13

13a. Head pattern posterior to eye comprised only of longitudinal
    stripes extending onto neck..14

13b. Head pattern posterior to eye includes a spot or horizontally
    oriented stripe or bar in addition to longitudinal stripes.....15

14a. Prominent red or orange stripe behind eye; plastron with
    single dark spot or smudge per scute (head striping may be
    obscure in old dark males but some plastral spots typically
    remain)...Slider

14b. All head stripes yellow; plastron with little or no pattern.......
    ....River Cooter

15a. Yellowish spot or comma-shaped marking behind eye;
    median keel of carapace low and lacking prominent knobs
    ....Common Map Turtle

15b. Conspicuous blotch, crescent, or horizontally oriented stripe
    or bar behind eye; median keel of carapace topped with low
    black knobs on vertebral scutes 2–4....................................16

16a. Broad squarish to rectangular blotch or bar behind eye; spot under eye and spot on lower jaw with a diameter > iris (Fig. 19a)..Ouachita Map Turtle

16b. Narrow stripe or crescent behind eye; if present, spot under eye and spot on lower jaw with a diameter < iris (Fig.19b) ....False Map Turtle

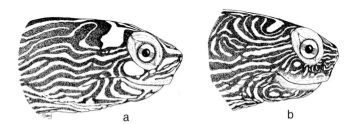

Figure 19. Head patterns of false map turtles: (a) Ouachita map turtle, (b) false map turtle.

ADULT LIZARD KEY

1a. Legs absent; a groove on each side of the body from neck to vent..Slender Glass Lizard

1b. Four limbs present; no groove on side of body......................2

2a. Scales strongly keeled making skin appear and feel rough...... ....Fence Lizard

2b. Scales not keeled...3

3a. Dorsal scales small and granular...4
3b. Dorsal scales large and smooth..5

4a. Belly with large transverse scales (Fig. 20); back with six longitudinal stripes; neck without black collar...................... ....Six-lined Racerunner

4b. Belly scales and back scales same size; back without longitudinal stripes; neck with black collar...Collared Lizard

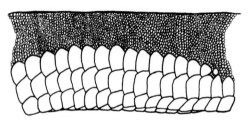

Figure 20. Ventral view of six-lined racerunner showing large transverse scales.

5a. Frontal scale not rectangular (Fig. 21a); lower eyelids with a transparent "window"; snout-vent length < 55 mm................ ....Ground Skink

5b. Frontal scale more or less rectangular (Fig. 21b); lower eyelids without a transparent "window"; snout-vent length > 55 mm...6

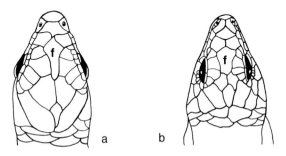

Figure 21. Dorsal view of skink heads: (a) V-shaped frontal scale (f) of ground skink; (b) rectangular frontal scale (f) of skinks.

6a. Postlabial scales 1 (Fig. 22a); supralabial scales usually 8 (Fig. 22a)..Broadhead Skink

6b. Postlabial scales 2 (Fig. 22b); supralabial scales usually 7 (Fig. 22b)..Five-lined Skink

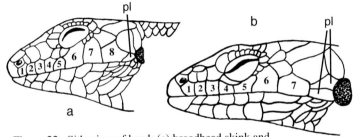

Figure 22. Side view of head: (a) broadhead skink and (b) five-lined skink showing position of postlabial scales (pl) and position of supralabial scales (numbered).

44

ADULT SNAKE KEY

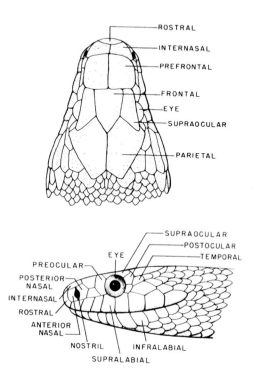

Figure 23. Dorsal and lateral apsects of snake heads showing scales.

1a. Pit between eye and nostril on each side of head; most scales on underside of tail in a single row (Fig. 24a)........................2

1b. Pit between eye and nostril absent; scales on underside of tail in 2 rows (Fig. 24b)...5

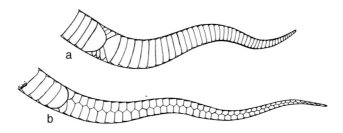

Figure 24. Ventral view of snakes: (a) single row of subcaudal scales, (b) double row of subcaudal scales.

2a. Tail ending in rattle or horny button; tail tip not yellow........3

2b. Tail not ending in rattle or horny button; tail tip yellow in juveniles..4

3a. Four large scales on top of head in front of eyes (Fig. 25a).....
....Massasauga

3b. Numerous small scales on top of head in front of eyes (Fig. 25b)...Timber Rattlesnake

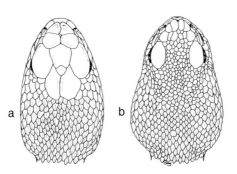

Figure 25. Top of head: (a) massasauga, (b) timber rattlesnake.

4a. Back with dark brown, hourglass-shaped saddles; head without black stripe behind each eye; upper lip without white line..Copperhead

4b. Back markings, if present, faint or obscured by dark brown or black ground color; head with black stripe behind each eye; upper lip with white line..............................Cottonmouth

5a. Some or all dorsal scales keeled (Fig. 26a)...........................6

5b. All scales smooth (Fig. 26b)..29

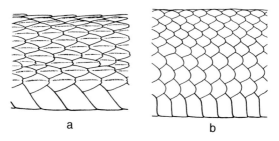

Figure 26. Side view of snakes: (a) keeled scales, (b) smooth scales.

6a. Anal plate divided (Fig. 27a)..7

6b. Anal plate entire (Fig. 27b)..23

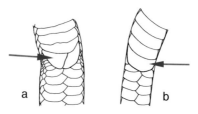

Figure 27. Ventral view of snake tails: (a) anal plate divided, (b) anal plate entire.

7a. Rostral scale (Fig. 23) upturned and keeled............................8

7b. Rostral scale (Fig. 23) not upturned or keeled.......................9

8a. Rostral scale (Fig. 23) pointed and only slightly upturned;
     underside of tail lighter than rest of belly..............................
     ....Eastern Hognose Snake

8b. Rostral scale (Fig. 23) strongly upturned; underside of tail as
     dark as rest of belly...........................Western Hognose Snake

9a. Loreal scale absent (Fig. 28a)...10

9b. Loreal scale present (Fig. 28b)...11

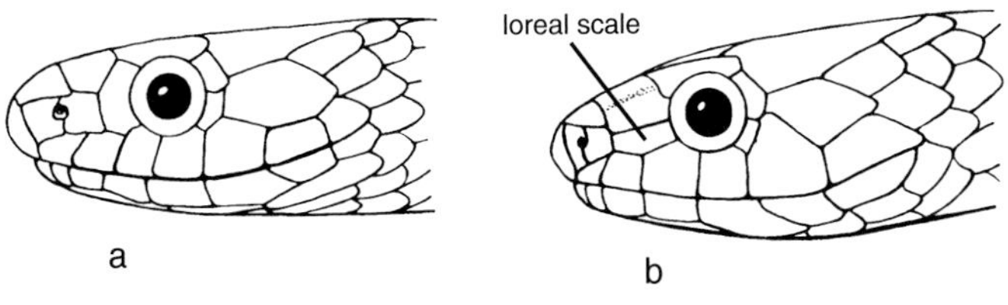

Figure 28. Side view of head: (a) brown snake showing loreal scale absent; (b) smooth earth snake showing loreal scale present.

10a. Dorsal scale rows at midbody (Fig. 29) 15; light spots on
     rear of head; belly orange or red....................Redbelly Snake

10b. Dorsal scale rows at midbody (Fig. 29) 17; light spots on
     head only in juveniles; belly white or pink........Brown Snake

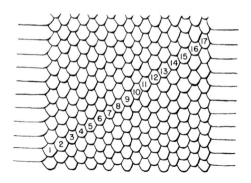

Figure 29. Dorsal view of snake body illustrating method of counting dorsal scale rows.

11a. Internasal scale 1 (Fig. 30a) [supralabials 6 on each side of head; postoculars 2 on each side of head; dorsal scales may be only weakly keeled]...........................Smooth Earth Snake

11b. Internasal scales 2 (Fig. 30b)..12

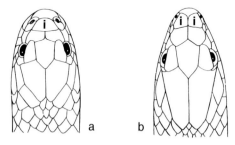

Figure 30. Dorsal view of head: (a) mud snake showing 1 internasal scale (i); (b) smooth green snake showing 2 internasal scales (i).

12a. Dorsal scale rows at midbody 17 (Fig. 29); dorsal color green..Rough Green Snake

12b. Dorsal scale rows (Fig. 29) more than 17; dorsal color not green...13

13a. Dorsal scales weakly keeled; postocular scales (Fig. 23) 2; dorsal scale rows (Fig. 29) 25–33.......................................14

13b. Dorsal scales strongly keeled (Fig. 26a); postocular scales (Fig. 23) 2 or 3; dorsal scale rows (Fig. 29) 25 or fewer....16

14a. Head gray with reddish brown spearpoint marking between eyes; belly pattern white with small gray squares...................
....Corn Snake

14b. No marking between eyes; belly pattern not as above........15

15a. Belly pattern yellow with large dark brown squares; ventral scales (Fig. 31) less than 220...............................Fox Snake

15b. Belly pattern black-and-white checkerboard anteriorly; ventral scales (Fig. 31) more than 220...................Rat Snake

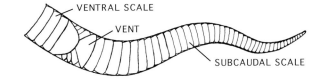

Figure 31. Underside of tail of snake showing the difference between ventral and subcaudal scales.

16a. Dorsal scale rows at midbody (Fig. 29) number 19............17

16b. Dorsal scale rows at midbody (Fig. 29) number more than 19..19

17a. Back with 4 rows of black spots; belly pink or reddish with a row of black spots along each side; preocular scales (Fig. 23) 1 on each side of head............................Kirtland's Snake

17b. Back without dark spots; belly plain or striped anteriorly and not red; preocular scales (Fig. 23) 2 on each side of head..18

18a. Belly entirely yellow or yellow with 1 thin median stripe...... ....Graham's Crayfish Snake

18b. Belly entirely dark brown or brown with 2 median stripes..... ....Queen Snake

19a. Dorsal scale rows at midbody (Fig. 29) 27 to 33 20

19b. Dorsal scale rows at midbody (Fig. 29) 25 or fewer...........21

20a. Subocular scales 1 or 2 (Fig. 32a); back dark olive-brown; belly dark with light spots.....Mississippi Green Water Snake

20b. Subocular scales absent (Fig. 32b); back with chainlike pattern; belly yellow with dark spots...................................... ....Diamondback Water Snake

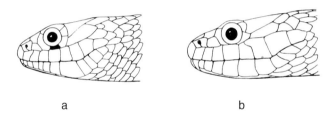

a   b

Figure 32. Side view of head: (a) Mississippi green water snake showing subocular scale (darkened); (b) diamondback water snake showing lack of subocular scales.

21a. Belly yellow or red with no markings.....................................
....Plainbelly Water Snake

21b. Belly marked with black or brown spots or blotches..........22

22a. Dorsal bands fewer than 20; belly light-yellow with
       irregular reddish brown markings......Southern Water Snake

22b. Dorsal bands more than 20; belly light-yellow with small
       red or brown spots or half-moons......Northern Water Snake

23a. Dorsal scale rows at mid-body (Fig. 29) 27 or more; back
       boldly blotched; prefrontal scales (Fig. 23) 3 or more;
       longitudinal stripes absent.......................................Bullsnake

23b. Dorsal scale rows at mid-body (Fig. 29) fewer than 27; back
       without blotches; prefrontal scales (Fig. 23) 2; longitudinal
       stripes usually present...24

24a. Infralabial scales (Fig. 23) 8 or more..................................25

24b. Infralabial scales (Fig. 23) fewer than 8..............................28

25a. Lateral stripe not touching fourth scale row; parietal scales (Fig. 23) without light spots...............Common Garter Snake

25b. Lateral stripe on fourth scale row, at least anteriorly; parietal scales (Fig. 23) with light spot in each................................26

26a. Stout-bodied; tail length usually less than 27% of total length; supralabial scales (Fig. 23) with black bars................ ....Plains Garter Snake

26b. Slender-bodied; tail usually 27% or more of total length; supralabial scales (Fig. 23) without black bars...................27

27a. Parietal scales (Fig. 23) with large, bright spots that usually touch each other; supralabial scales (Fig. 23) usually 8; brown lateral stripe absent.................Western Ribbon Snake

27b. Parietal scales (Fig. 23) with faint spots that never touch each other; supralabial scales (Fig. 23) usually 7; brown lateral stripe on first scale row extends slightly onto belly..... ....Eastern Ribbon Snake

28a. Back and belly unmarked; [dorsal scales may be only weakly keeled].......................................Smooth Earth Snake

28b. Back with longitudinal light stripes; belly with 2 rows of black spots down the center................................Lined Snake

29a. Anal plate divided (Fig. 27a)..30

29b. Anal plate entire (Fig. 27b)..37

30a. Neck with light-colored ring........................Ringneck Snake

30b. Neck without light-colored ring..31

31a. Dorsal scale rows at midbody (Fig. 29) 15 or fewer...........32

31b. Dorsal scale rows at midbody (Fig. 29) 17 or more............34

32a. Dorsal scale rows at midbody (Fig. 29) 13; [dark dorsal color in strong contrast to pink belly]...............Worm Snake

32b. Dorsal scale rows at midbody (Fig. 29) 15.........................33

33a. Loreal scale absent (Fig. 28a); back tan; belly salmon-pink; head flattened and usually darker than body..Flathead Snake

33b. Loreal scale present (Fig. 28b); back grass-green; belly yellow; head not flattened nor darker than body.....................
....Smooth Green Snake

34a. Dorsal scale rows at midbody (Fig. 29) 19; belly black with transverse red bands; tail ending in a horny tip...............
....Mud Snake

34b. Dorsal scale rows at midbody (Fig. 29) 17; belly without red bands; tail not ending in a horny tip..............................35

35a. Preocular scale (Fig. 23) absent [usually six supralabial scales; belly white or cream, some dorsal scales may be weakly keeled]..Smooth Earth Snake

35b. Preocular scale (Fig. 23) present..36

36a. Dorsal scale rows (Fig. 29) 15 at posterior end of body; back coloration uniform and varies from black to green; belly white or cream; tail scales not patterned like a braided whip ....Racer

36b. Dorsal scale rows (Fig. 29) 13 or fewer at posterior end of body; back coloration uniformly black; belly uniformly black, becoming lighter under tail; tail scales patterned like a braided whip..Coachwhip

37a. Dorsal pattern of white or yellow dots on black groundcolor ....Common Kingsnake

37b. Dorsal pattern of distinct dark blotches on light groundcolor 38

38a. Belly unmarked; snout pointed...........................Scarlet Snake

38b. Belly marked; snout not pointed...39

39a. Dorsal scale rows at midbody (Fig. 29) 25 or 27; ventral spots gray and indistinct against the greenish yellow background; borders of dorsal blotches narrower than half a scale length..Prairie Kingsnake

39b. Dorsal scale rows at midbody (Fig. 29) usually 21; ventral spots black and in sharp contrast to the white background; borders of dorsal blotches almost as wide as the length of one scale..Milk Snake

Species Accounts

ORDER CAUDATA — SALAMANDERS

Twenty species of salamanders, representing six families, occur in Illinois. They are secretive, being most active at night, and may be the least observed of the state's amphibians and reptiles. Although resembling lizards in body form (head, trunk, tail, usually four legs), salamanders live in water or in cool, high-humidity environments in or near the ground where they feed on a variety of other small animals. Salamander skin is thin, scaleless, and covered with a layer of moisture secreted by glands.

The hellbender (family Cryptobranchidae), mudpuppy (family Proteidae), and lesser siren (family Sirenidae) spend their entire lives in lakes, ponds, permanent streams, or swamps where they sometimes are encountered by fishermen. The eastern newt (family Salamandridae) is peculiar in having three life stages: adults that live and breed in lakes and ponds, aquatic larvae, and a terrestrial juvenile stage called the eft. The eight species of mole salamanders (family Ambystomatidae) live in and under rotting logs and in burrows in the forest floor, emerging, usually at night, during heavy rain and during the annual breeding season. Adults sometimes are observed crossing highways as they migrate to breeding ponds on rainy spring or autumn nights. They court and deposit eggs in ponds and temporary pools where their larvae can be found feeding and growing during spring and early summer. The remaining eight terrestrial or streamside species, the lungless salamanders (family Plethodontidae), seldom are active on the surface of the ground except at night, usually following rain. Because they respire through their skin and dry out easily, these animals live mostly under moist leaves, logs, and rocks, or in burrows in the ground. Some lungless salamanders are more common around caves, springs, or spring-fed streams (cave, four-toed, longtail); some along banks of small, rocky streams (dusky, southern two-lined); and others in forest floor litter (redback, zigzag, slimy).

Most adult salamanders are relatively easy to identify by distinctive coloration or pigment distribution, number of legs and toes, presence or absence of a nasolabial groove, presence and number of costal grooves, and body proportions. However, larvae and juveniles can be difficult to identify immediately after metamorphosis. Sometimes larvae are best identified by allowing them to transform and develop adult coloration.

Four salamanders have very limited distributions within Illinois: the silvery salamander is a biologically peculiar all-female species known from only one natural population; the dusky salamander occurs in only two counties; the four-toed salamander is a relic from an earlier climatic era; and the hellbender was, until recently, considered extirpated from the state. Many populations of other species have been eliminated, reduced, or fragmented through loss of habitat: draining of wetlands, channelizing of streams, reduction of temporary ponds and sloughs, and clearing of forests.

In the species accounts that follow, size is given in "cm TL," which is the straight line length from the tip of the nose to the end of the tail, given in centimeters. The maximum size listed in the "Description" section for each species is the greatest TL recorded for specimens in Illinois unless otherwise stated.

Jefferson salamander   **Ambystomatidae**
Ambystoma jeffersonianum

Key Characters: Long, slender toes; broad snout; no nasolabial grooves; wide head; belly paler than sides and back; cloacal opening surrounded by gray.

Similar Species: Blue-spotted salamander, silvery salamander, slimy salamander, smallmouth salamander.

Description: A long (up to 17 cm TL), brown or dark gray salamander with spindly limbs. Head distinctly wider than those of blue-spotted and smallmouth salamanders, snout relatively longer and broader, and legs and toes longer. Adpressed limbs overlap by 2–4 costal folds. Costal grooves 12–13. Cloacal walls of breeding male greatly swollen with glands that produce spermatophores. Larva has a large head, unpigmented throat, long, slender toes, and intensively pigmented tail fin.

Habitat: Upland deciduous forest, especially beech-maple forests of extreme eastern Illinois.

Natural History: Subterranean adults are seldom seen outside of the breeding season, but may occasionally be found in leaf litter or under logs. Diet includes beetles, centipedes, slugs, worms, and other invertebrates. During February–March rains, adults migrate several hundred meters to congregate and breed in scattered vernal woodland ponds or fish-free permanent ponds. The 180–210 eggs (2-2.5 mm diameter) enclosed within jelly-like masses (usually 14-22 eggs per mass) are attached to twigs and stems in water. Eggs hatch in less than a month and larvae remain in pond 2–3 months where they prey on invertebrates and other amphibian larvae. Predators of adults include skunks, raccoons, and snakes.

Status: Threatened in Illinois. First found in Illinois in 1990, known to occur at only a few localities in the Wabash Border Division (Fig. 1).

Jefferson salamander (*Ambystoma jeffersonianum*), Edgar Co., IL. (MR)

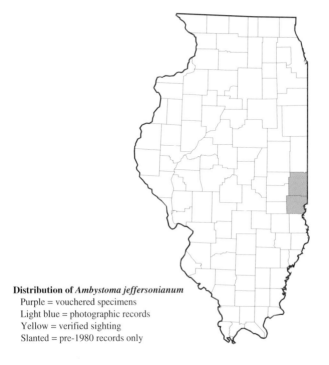

Distribution of *Ambystoma jeffersonianum*
  Purple = vouchered specimens
  Light blue = photographic records
  Yellow = verified sighting
  Slanted = pre-1980 records only

Blue-spotted salamander   **Ambystomatidae**
Ambystoma laterale

Key Characters: White and blue flecks on body; cloacal opening surrounded by black; no nasolabial grooves.

Similar Species: Jefferson salamander, silvery salamander, slimy salamander, smallmouth salamander.

Description: A medium-sized (up to 13 cm TL), nondescript dark salamander with small white, gray, or bluish flecks on back or sides. Spots and flecks fewer on back, more numerous on lower sides. Smaller, darker, and more spotted than Jefferson and silvery salamanders, with narrower snout and shorter legs. Adpressed limbs overlap 1–2 costal folds. Larva is dark brown with yellowish back blotches and a yellow side stripe.

Habitat: Northern swamp white oak flatwoods and mesic maple-basswood forests containing temporary or fish-free breeding ponds. Also in floodplain forests, oak savannas, pine plantations, marshes, and miscellaneous second-growth forests.

Natural History: Adults occur under logs and other cover during much of year. Diet includes beetles, centipedes, slugs, worms, and other invertebrates. Reproductive biology similar to Jefferson salamander except that *A. laterale* breeds in more open sites and females attach their small (1.5–1.7 mm diameter) eggs singly or in masses of up to 4 on edges of leaves and other debris on pond bottom; sometimes eggs are scattered.

Status: Locally abundant in relatively undisturbed areas of the Northeastern Morainal Division (Fig. 1). Greatest threat is urban sprawl.

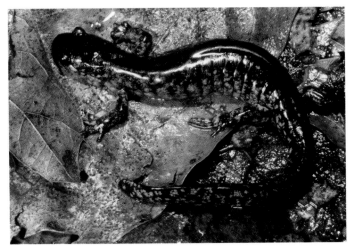

Blue-spotted salamander (*Ambystoma laterale*), Will Co., IL. (MR)

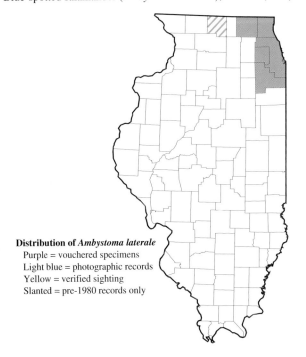

Distribution of *Ambystoma laterale*
Purple = vouchered specimens
Light blue = photographic records
Yellow = verified sighting
Slanted = pre-1980 records only

Spotted salamander   **Ambystomatidae**
Ambystoma maculatum

Key Characters: Two rows of yellow or orange-yellow spots down back from behind eye nearly to tail tip; belly slate gray or black, sometimes with small white flecks.

Similar Species: Tiger salamander.

Description: Stout salamander up to 19 cm TL with bright yellow spots on back and occasionally orange spots on head. Rarely without spots, but unspotted individuals still recognizable by robust build and plain belly. Adpressed limbs usually do not meet, except in juveniles, which have proportionally longer legs. Female 5%–7% longer TL than male but with proportionally shorter tail. Larva uniformly brown, never with dark blotches on back.

Habitat: Deciduous forests with access to vernal pools or fish-free permanent ponds suitable for breeding and larval life.

Natural History: Largely subterranean adults and juveniles are found in burrows, under or in large logs, and under large rocks, where they eat a variety of invertebrates including earthworms, snails, slugs, spiders, millipedes, and insects. They have been observed feeding at night at the mouths of burrows. Reproductive biology similar to Jefferson salamander except that *A. maculatum* females attach their eggs in dense gelatinous masses of up to 200 on edges of leaves, twigs, and other debris on pond bottom. The synchronous early spring migration of adults to breeding ponds is impressive. Predators of adults include skunks, raccoons, and snakes.

Status: Southern and eastern populations are separated from those in the north by the Grand Prairie Division (Fig. 1). Although locally common in some areas, continuing forest fragmentation could isolate some populations from suitable breeding ponds.

Spotted salamander (*Ambystoma maculatum*), Jackson Co., IL. (MR)

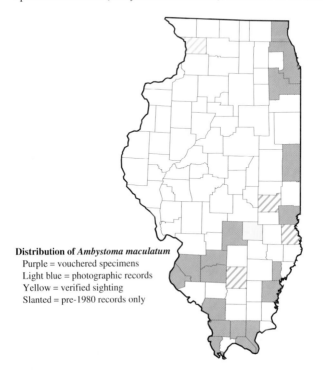

Distribution of *Ambystoma maculatum*
Purple = vouchered specimens
Light blue = photographic records
Yellow = verified sighting
Slanted = pre-1980 records only

Marbled salamander   **Ambystomatidae**
Ambystoma opacum

Key Characters: Stocky, black or gray body with whitish crossbands on back and tail; belly black, sometimes with white flecks.

Similar Species: Adults not likely to be confused with any other salamander.

Description: Short (up to 12 cm TL), stocky salamander with grayish white (female) or bright white (male) crossbands on back and tail, sometimes incomplete, sometimes running together along sides. Before banded pattern develops on juveniles, the back is covered with scattered whitish or silvery frosting. Male has more protuberant cloacal region than female, especially during breeding season. Larva distinguished by uniform dark stippling on throat and sides of belly, and row of conspicuous clear spots on midsides.

Habitat: Mesic forests, dry hillsides, and moist floodplains. In autumn, adults migrate to wooded breeding areas, where they mate in dry pond basins or margins of ponds and swamps that will be flooded by autumn or winter rains.

Natural History: The largely subterranean adults are sometimes found under rocks and logs, especially during September–October, when they breed in dry pond basins. Each female lays 100–300 eggs in a loose cluster on land and curls protectively around them. The eggs hatch when covered with water from autumn rains. Larvae feed on microcrustaceans, insect larvae, snails, isopods, amphipods, and other aquatic invertebrates and transform the following April or May. Adults feed on beetles, centipedes, slugs, worms, and other invertebrates.

Status: Much suitable habitat remains in counties south of the Shelbyville Moraine, and some along the Vermilion River.

Marbled salamander (*Ambystoma opacum*), Jackson Co., IL. (MR)

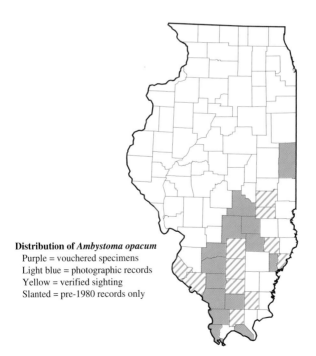

Distribution of *Ambystoma opacum*
  Purple = vouchered specimens
  Light blue = photographic records
  Yellow = verified sighting
  Slanted = pre-1980 records only

Silvery salamander
Ambystoma platineum

Ambystomatidae

Key Characters: Dark, slender body; all-female species.

Similar Species: Blue-spotted salamander, Jefferson salamander, slimy salamander, smallmouth salamander.

Description: A long (up to 17 cm TL) salamander with blue lichenlike markings on sides and scattered blue flecks over head, back, limbs, and belly. Juveniles more brightly marked with blue. Costal grooves usually 13 (80%), occasionally 14. Lower jaw does not protrude beyond upper. Silvery salamanders are distinguishable from Jefferson salamanders only by counting chromosomes or measuring the silvery's larger red blood cells.

Habitat: Vicinity of two shallow vernal ponds in a mesic oak-sugar maple-beech forest in Vermilion County.

Natural History: Thought to have originated through hybridization and backcrossing between *A. laterale* and *A. jeffersonianum* thousands of years ago, this unusual all-female species usually occurs with the Jefferson salamander. The single known Illinois population occurs with smallmouth, marbled, and spotted salamanders. During February and March rains, the subterranean adults migrate to ponds and breed. They use smallmouth salamander sperm to activate egg development. Jelly-covered masses of 2–50 eggs are attached to sticks or left loose on pond bottom. Mortality of developing embryos is sometimes as high as 80%. Adults feed on beetles, centipedes, slugs, worms, and other invertebrates.

Status: Endangered in Illinois. Distribution extremely limited in the state. Only one natural population is known, in a state park. In some years the breeding pond has not held water long enough for larvae to develop to metamorphosis.

Silvery salamander (*Ambystoma platineum*), Vermilion Co., IL. (RAB)

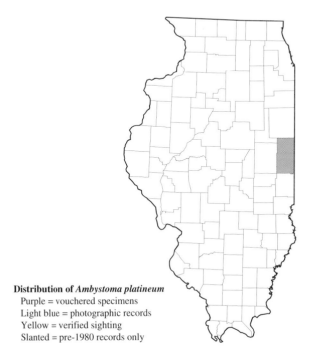

Distribution of *Ambystoma platineum*
  Purple = vouchered specimens
  Light blue = photographic records
  Yellow = verified sighting
  Slanted = pre-1980 records only

Mole salamander   **Ambystomatidae**
Ambystoma talpoideum

Key Characters: Dark, short body with disproportionately large head.

Similar Species: Smallmouth salamander.

Description: A stocky, gray to brownish black salamander up to 11 cm TL. Usually conspicuous light and dark stripes on the belly, even of larva. Often a white edge along top of adult tail. Costal grooves 10–11. Larva distinctively marked with mottled throat, pale streak on side of head, dark stripe extending down middle of belly, and pale stripe on lower side.

Habitat: Bald cypress and tupelo swamplands, sloughs, and nearby ponds of the Cache, Mississippi, and Ohio river valleys at the southern tip of Illinois.

Natural History: Adults move to breeding ponds (vernal pools, fish-free ponds, or swamp edges) for courtship and egg-laying during late autumn and winter rains. Females attach 200–400 small (2 mm diameter) eggs, in jelly-covered clusters of 1–35 each, to twigs and leaves under water. Larvae transform during summer or autumn and, in a few permanent ponds, some large larvae are known to overwinter. Adults feed on beetles, centipedes, slugs, worms, and other invertebrates.

Status: This salamander has a small range in the state, and requires wet bottomland and swamp habitat, much of which has been drained and fragmented. It is locally common in some of the remaining habitat fragments protected in state conservation areas, nature preserves, and Cypress Creek National Wildlife Refuge.

Mole salamander (*Ambystoma talpoideum*), Alexander Co., IL. (MR)

Distribution of *Ambystoma talpoideum*
  Purple = vouchered specimens
  Light blue = photographic records
  Yellow = verified sighting
  Slanted = pre-1980 records only

Smallmouth salamander   **Ambystomatidae**
Ambystoma texanum

Key Characters: Small head; short, narrow snout; protruding lower jaw.

Similar Species: Blue-spotted salamander, mole salamander, Jefferson salamander, silvery salamander, slimy salamander.

Description: A medium-sized (up to 17 cm TL) salamander with lichenlike gray markings along sides. Costal grooves 14–16. Limbs and toes relatively short. Adpressed limbs usually separated by 2–4 costal folds. In contrast to single tooth rows in other Illinois *Ambystoma*, *A. texanum* has 2–3 maxillary tooth rows, one behind the other.

Habitat: Widespread in poorly drained woodlands, prairies, pastures, and even cultivated or urban areas where breeding ponds remain. Most prevalent under logs and occasionally in excavated crayfish burrows and drainage tiles. Adults are occasionally found on rocky hillsides.

Natural History: Adults are subterranean outside of breeding season and migrate to breeding ponds (fish-free ponds, drainage ditches, vernal woodland pools, low, flooded places in cultivated fields) from January to March (April in northern counties) during prolonged rain. Eggs have even been found in cisterns. Several hundred small eggs (2 mm diameter) are deposited in masses of 6–30, attached to sticks and vegetation in water. Depending on when eggs were laid, larvae transform May through July. Adults eat earthworms, slugs, and various arthropods.

Status: Common and widespread. Greatest threat is loss of wet areas for breeding and larval development.

Smallmouth salamander (*Ambystoma texanum*), Jackson Co., IL. (MR)

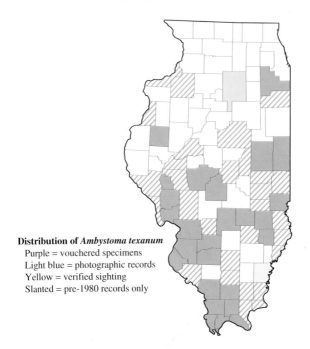

Distribution of *Ambystoma texanum*
 Purple = vouchered specimens
 Light blue = photographic records
 Yellow = verified sighting
 Slanted = pre-1980 records only

Tiger salamander   **Ambystomatidae**
Ambystoma tigrinum

Key Characters: Large head; dark body marked with irregular yellow spots or blotches, some extending onto belly.

Similar Species: Spotted salamander.

Subspecies: Eastern tiger salamander, *A. t. tigrinum*.

Description: The largest terrestrial salamander in Illinois (up to 33 cm TL). Pattern varies from dark background and small yellow spots (juvenile) to large fused spots and blotches obscuring background (old adult). Hatchling larva lacks balancers and is yellow to tan with paired black blotches on back. Older larva has wide head, pale underside, and toes with broad, flat bases; occasional overwintering larva reaches adult size.

Habitat: Forests, woodlands, pastures, orchards, prairies, and cultivated fields. Tolerant of habitat disturbance within towns and cities, as long as breeding ponds remain.

Natural History: Adults live in burrows and under logs, rocks, and other cover and move about the surface at night especially after rain and during winter and spring breeding migration. Fish-free ponds are required for breeding and larval life. During February–April, females attach eggs to twigs, leaves, and plant stems under water in jelly-covered clusters of 20–50. Larvae grow fast and are important pond predators. Larvae transform in late summer or autumn. Adults feed on beetles, centipedes, slugs, worms, and other invertebrates.

Status: Locally common. Persists but is not abundant where disturbed by agriculture and urban development. Imported larvae often sold as fish bait under the erroneous name "waterdogs."

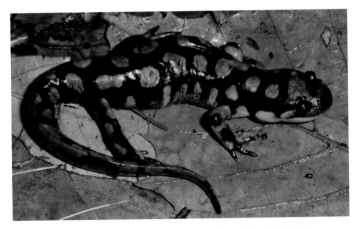

Tiger salamander (*Ambystoma tigrinum*), Jackson Co., IL. (MR)

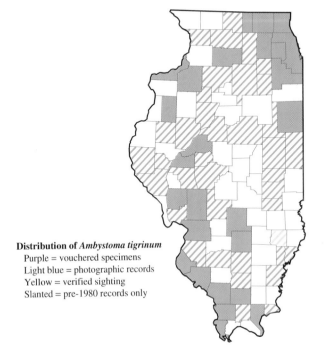

Distribution of *Ambystoma tigrinum*
  Purple = vouchered specimens
  Light blue = photographic records
  Yellow = verified sighting
  Slanted = pre-1980 records only

Hellbender
Cryptobranchidae

Cryptobranchus alleganiensis

Key Characters: Broad, flattened head and body; small lidless eyes; single circular gill opening on each side; wrinkled skin folds along sides and from trailing edges of legs.

Similar Species: Mudpuppy, large tiger salamander larvae.

Subspecies: Eastern hellbender, *C. a. alleganiensis*.

Description: A large (up to 44 cm TL), wrinkled salamander with yellowish brown to brownish black head and body, often with darker spots and mottling. Costal grooves inconspicuous, nearly hidden within skin wrinkles. Occasionally one gill opening is missing. Legs are short and stout; the hind foot has 5 toes. Tail compressed and keeled (adults) or finned (larvae) to the pelvis. Spotted larvae hatch at about 30 mm TL and transform 11–13 cm TL.

Habitat: Fast-flowing rivers and large creeks, especially rocky shoals. Cavities under submerged rocks and logs are important as nest sites and daytime retreats.

Natural History: Adults seldom seen except in clear water or when caught in commercial fishing nets. Adults eat crayfish, small fish, snails, insects, worms, and tadpoles. Reproduction occurs from August into October. Female lays 250–450 eggs in long beaded strings in gravel depressions excavated by male under large submerged rock or log. Male releases sperm over eggs in nest and remains to protect them during development. Slimy skin secretions are toxic and probably repel predatory fish. The only predator of large adults is man.

Status: Endangered in Illinois. Most former rocky habitat has been buried under silt.

Hellbender (*Cryptobranchus alleganiensis*), Missouri. (ER)

Distribution of *Cryptobranchus alleganiensis*
   Purple = vouchered specimens
   Light blue = photographic records
   Yellow = verified sighting
   Slanted = pre-1980 records only

Dusky salamander   **Plethodontidae**
Desmognathus fuscus

Key Characters: Nasolabial grooves present; pale diagonal line from eye to angle of jaw.

Similar Species: Four-toed salamander, smallmouth salamander, southern two-lined salamander.

Subspecies: Spotted dusky salamander, *D. f. conanti*.

Description: A moderately stout (up to 12 cm TL) salamander with dark markings on back, remnants of spotted juvenile pattern, that form a broad, irregular light stripe down back and onto tail. Light belly is mottled with black and light flecks. Male has enlarged jaw muscles during spring/summer breeding season. Larva with short, glistening-white gills, and 5–8 pairs of light spots on back.

Habitat: Cool, spring-fed headwater streams flowing through forests. Larvae are found in streams and spring seeps.

Natural History: Adults are mainly nocturnal, moving about on stream banks at night. During the day they take refuge in burrows or under logs, rocks, and leaves at edge of the stream. Adults eat a variety of invertebrates and occasionally their own larvae. The tail is easily broken; many adults have short or regenerated tails as evidence of escape from predators. Mating occurs from April through July. The female curls around and guards her eggs, which are laid in a burrow, moss, or depression under log, rock, or leaves near water. Larvae hatch in autumn and wriggle into water, where they feed and grow until transforming the following spring.

Status: Endangered in Illinois. Occurs only in isolated populations in Pulaski County, and one (probably an introduction) in Johnson County.

Dusky salamander (*Desmognathus fuscus*), Pulaski Co., IL. (RAB)

Distribution of *Desmognathus fuscus*
Purple = vouchered specimens
Light blue = photographic records
Yellow = verified sighting
Slanted = pre-1980 records only

Southern two-lined salamander   Plethodontidae
Eurycea cirrigera

Key Characters: Slender yellow or tan body with 2 dark stripes down back from eyes onto tail.

Similar Species: Cave salamander, longtail salamander, dusky salamander.

Description: A small (up to 11 cm TL), slender salamander with small black spots between the dark back stripes and on top of head. Belly unspotted yellow. Tail 61% of TL or less and legs short. Costal grooves distinct. Nasolabial grooves present and, in breeding male, continue onto elongated cirri on upper lip. Three or more costal folds between adpressed limbs. Larva slender, with low tail fin and long gill rami, unpigmented throat, and marked on the back with paired light spots that sometimes fuse with narrow midback pale stripe.

Habitat: Near rocky brooks, spring seeps, and spring-fed streams in mesic forests.

Natural History: Adults can be found along edge, larvae in pools. They eat worms and other small invertebrates. At night during rain, adults and juveniles wander into woods as they feed. Slippery and agile, they escape by quickly swimming, jumping, or running to cover. From April to May, females attach white eggs, individually in tight clusters, to undersides of rocks that are exposed to running water. Larvae probably transform during second year of life.

Status: Locally abundant in spring and autumn. Western edge of range ends along the Kankakee River, eastern edge of the Grand Prairie, and in the eastern Shawnee and Cretaceous Hills (Fig. 1).

Southern two-lined salamander (*Eurycea cirrigera*), Will Co., IL. (MR)

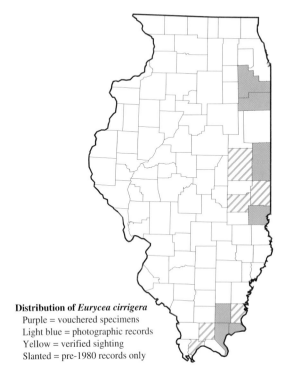

Distribution of *Eurycea cirrigera*
  Purple = vouchered specimens
  Light blue = photographic records
  Yellow = verified sighting
  Slanted = pre-1980 records only

Longtail salamander
Eurycea longicauda

Plethodontidae

Key Characters: Slender yellow or orange body; sides of long, slender tail with dark vertical bars or uniformly black.

Similar Species: Cave salamander, southern two-lined salamander.

Subspecies: Longtail salamander, *E. l. longicauda*; dark-sided salamander, *E. l. melanopleura*.

Description: A long (up to 16 cm TL), slender lemon-yellow to yellowish orange salamander with scattered black blotches along back and sides. Belly yellow to cream and usually unspotted. Costal grooves and nasolabial grooves present. *Eurycea l. melanopleura* is more darkly pigmented, with yellow-green to yellow-brown ground coloring and sides of body and tail uniformly dark. Larva slender with low tail fin, long gill branches, dark flecks on the anterior third of throat, and broad pale stripe down back.

Habitat: Near cool streams and spring seeps in forests of dissected, rocky uplands and valley edges. Dark-sided subspecies partial to twilight zones of caves, sometimes deep within caves and along surface streams nearby.

Natural History: Adults emerge from rocky refugia at night, especially after rain, and feed on terrestrial insects, spiders, centipedes, snails, and earthworms. They are sometimes seen on tree trunks, damp leaves, rock faces, or even on roads during these forays. Eggs laid in wet underground crevices in late summer or autumn. Hatchlings appear in late winter or early spring and larvae transform in summer.

Status: Locally abundant.

Longtail salamander (*Eurycea longicauda*), Jackson Co., IL. (MR)

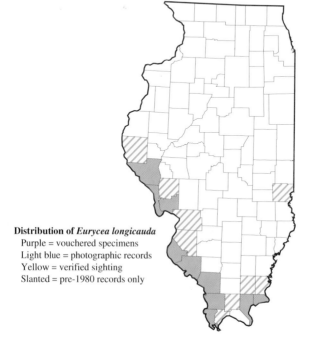

Distribution of *Eurycea longicauda*
Purple = vouchered specimens
Light blue = photographic records
Yellow = verified sighting
Slanted = pre-1980 records only

Cave salamander   Plethodontidae
Eurycea lucifuga

Key Characters: Bright orange or reddish orange body; large eyes; black spots on sides of tail scattered rather than arranged into vertical bars.

Similar Species: Longtail salamander.

Description: A very long (up to 18 cm TL) salamander with a wide head and scattered black spots or blotches forming no pattern anywhere on body. Belly unspotted and pale yellowish. Mature male has a mental hedonic gland at the tip of the lower jaw and swollen cirri at the ends of nasolabial grooves. Larva slender, with low tail fin and long gill rami, darkly pigmented on anterior half of throat, and with a broad pale stripe down back. Recently transformed juvenile has shorter tail and is more yellow, closely resembling longtails; check differences in throat and tail pigment.

Habitat: Twilight zone of limestone caves and limestone crevices offer optimal habitat. Also found deeper within caves, and under rocks, logs, and plant debris in woodlands near caves, and around spring-fed swamps.

Natural History: Nocturnal juveniles and adults are found on damp rock walls and ledges, sometimes in large numbers. Diet includes slugs, worms, and a wide variety of insects and other arthropods. Large (5 mm diameter) pale eggs are attached to rocks in cave and underground spring pools in autumn and winter. Most hatchlings are washed out into springs and streams where they grow to transformation.

Status: Locally abundant throughout limestone regions of the Shawnee Hills and Lower Mississippi Border Divisions (Fig. 1).

Cave salamander (*Eurycea licifuga*), Pope Co., IL. (MR)

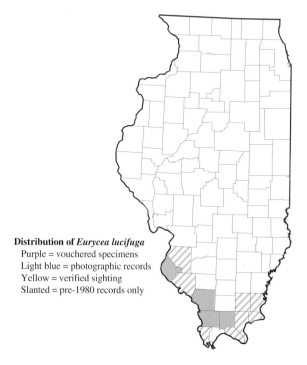

Distribution of *Eurycea lucifuga*
  Purple = vouchered specimens
  Light blue = photographic records
  Yellow = verified sighting
  Slanted = pre-1980 records only

Four-toed salamander

Plethodontidae

Hemidactylium scutatum

Key Characters: 4 rather than 5 toes on hind feet; circular constriction at base of tail.

Similar Species: Juvenile eastern newt, juvenile dusky salamander, redback salamander, zigzag salamander.

Description: A small (up to 10 cm TL), slender, reddish brown salamander with a black-spotted ivory-white belly. Costal grooves extend to midline of back. Snout distinctly pale brown. Some individuals have a broad pale brown stripe down midback. Tail breaks off easily.

Habitat: Boggy pools or spring-fed ravines in undisturbed or mature deciduous forests. Several localities are second-growth woods in soggy soil below dams of man-made lakes.

Natural History: Terrestrial adults occupy moist, rotten logs and feed on a variety of arthropods on forest floor. Mating occurs in autumn, before hibernation. During April–May, female broods 20–60 moderately large (2.5–3 mm diameter) eggs laid in a cavity a few inches above water within mats of moss or leaves, within logs, under rocks, or along spring-fed streams or pools. Within two months, hatchlings fall or wriggle into water where they develop into high-finned aquatic larvae.

Status: Threatened in Illinois. A few scattered localities are relics of post-glacial times when range was more continuous and northern forests covered much of Illinois. Populations in Cook and Lake counties probably extirpated by habitat destruction.

Four-toed salamander (*Hemidactylium scutatum*), Will Co., IL. (MR)

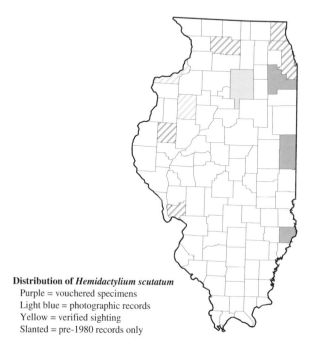

Distribution of *Hemidactylium scutatum*
  Purple = vouchered specimens
  Light blue = photographic records
  Yellow = verified sighting
  Slanted = pre-1980 records only

Redback salamander   **Plethodontidae**
Plethodon cinereus

Key Characters: 18–20 costal grooves; "salt and pepper" belly without orange marks.

Similar Species: Four-toed salamander, juvenile dusky salamander, zigzag salamander.

Description: A dark, slender salamander (up to 11 cm TL) with straight-edged reddish stripe on back. Belly mottled or dotted black and white but never has orange marks around bases of front legs. Costal grooves 18–20. Legs small and short, toes of adpressed limbs separated by 4–9 costal folds. Some proportion of individuals (up to 97% in Crawford County, but averaging less than 35% elsewhere) lack the back stripe and are uniformly dark gray to black (lead phase).

Habitat: Terrestrial. Found in forests under logs, bark, sticks, and stones.

Natural History: Completely terrestrial with no larval stage. Feeds on worms, small insects, and other arthropods. Eight to ten yellowish eggs are laid in a cluster under rocks, in rotten logs and tree stumps, or under moss or tree bark. Female guards eggs until they hatch into tiny juveniles in late summer. Hatchling may have a yolk sac and tiny gills for a day or two.

Status: Reaches western edge of range along the eastern forest/prairie border of Illinois. Very rare in northeastern counties because of habitat loss. Remains relatively common elsewhere.

Redback salamander (*Plethodon cinereus*), Cook Co., IL. (MR)

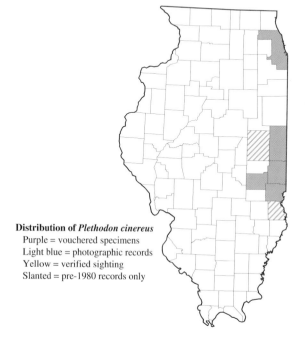

Distribution of *Plethodon cinereus*
Purple = vouchered specimens
Light blue = photographic records
Yellow = verified sighting
Slanted = pre-1980 records only

Zigzag salamander   **Plethodontidae**
Plethodon dorsalis

Key Characters: Reddish or yellowish back stripe broadly zig-zagged (east), or narrow and straight edged (west); orange marks around bases of front legs.

Similar Species: Four-toed salamander, juvenile dusky salamander, redback salamander.

Subspecies: Eastern zigzag salamander, *P. d. dorsalis*.

Description: A slender salamander (up to 11 cm TL) similar to the redback salamander, but not quite as dark. Costal grooves 17–18. Black and white belly markings. Striking geographic variation in back stripe that extends from head to tail tip: in eastern counties, it is a broad reddish (sometimes yellow) zigzag or has wavy edges; in some individuals, it is yellow, gray, or black. In counties bordering the Mississippi River, the back stripe is narrower, nearly straight sided, and either red or absent (lead phase).

Habitat: Moist, rocky forests. Seasonally abundant in woodlands around rocky springs and cave entrances.

Natural History: In late autumn and spring, during rainy periods, it may be abundant under rocks on forested hillsides. During mid-summer, individuals move deeper into soil, sometimes encountering moist cave passages where they accumulate in large numbers. Females have been observed brooding eggs in rock crevices in a southern Illinois cave June through September.

Status: No current concerns.

Zigzag salamander (*Plethodon dorsalis*), Pope Co., IL. (MR)

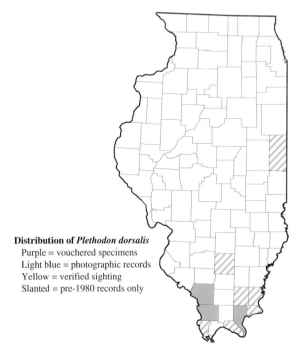

Distribution of *Plethodon dorsalis*
 Purple = vouchered specimens
 Light blue = photographic records
 Yellow = verified sighting
 Slanted = pre-1980 records only

Northern slimy salamander   **Plethodontidae**
Plethodon glutinosus

Key Characters: White or silvery dots and flecks scattered over the body, commonly concentrated along lower sides; nasolabial grooves present.

Similar Species: Blue-spotted salamander, Jefferson salamander, silvery salamander, smallmouth salamander.

Description: Medium-sized (up to 17 cm TL) salamander with black or bluish black back and uniform gray-black belly, sometimes with light flecks. Costal grooves 14–15. Tail long and circular in cross-section. Head relatively large. Adult male with a light circular hedonic gland under chin. Recently hatched juvenile may have short, white gills.

Habitat: Eastern deciduous forests under bark or other debris on ground, especially on hillsides.

Natural History: This completely terrestrial salamander can be found in burrows, under rocks, in and under logs, and in rotten tree stumps in spring and autumn, but disappears deeper into soil during summer and winter. It prowls the forest floor at night feeding on worms and arthropods. Copious, adhesive skin secretions provide protection from predators. Tiny hatchlings, which resemble adults in form and color, grow to become the largest completely terrestrial salamanders in Illinois. Females deposit and brood clusters of 10–20 large white eggs in damp rotten logs, burrows, or rock crevices. Brooding females were observed in rock crevices in a southern Illinois cave during October and November. The embryos hatched by May of the following year.

Status: Most commonly encountered woodland salamander in southern half of state.

Northern slimy salamander (*Plethodon glutinosus*), Jackson Co., IL. (MR)

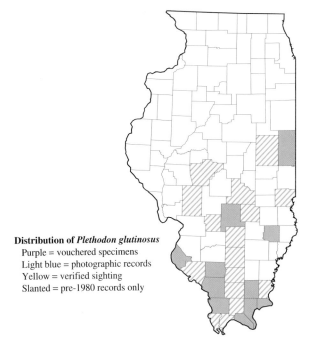

Distribution of *Plethodon glutinosus*
Purple = vouchered specimens
Light blue = photographic records
Yellow = verified sighting
Slanted = pre-1980 records only

Mudpuppy   **Proteidae**
Necturus maculosus

Key Characters: Bushy external gills; 4 toes on hind feet; dark stripe running through eye.

Similar Species: Hellbender, larval *Ambystoma*.

Subspecies: Mudpuppy, *N. m. maculosus*.

Description: Large (up to 34 cm TL), stout-bodied brownish gray, rust brown, or black salamander with scattered round black spots of various sizes. Costal grooves 15–16. Belly gray with dark spots, or plain gray. Snout blunt, head flattened and widest behind eyes. Tail short, tail fins not extending onto body. Larva and juvenile have broad dark stripes down back that are bordered on either side by yellow stripes.

Habitat: Lakes, ponds, rivers, and large creeks. More abundant in clear waters but can withstand turbid, mud-banked streams if gravel headwaters are available for reproduction.

Natural History: This totally harmless and attractive sala-mander is active year-round. Shelters by day in deeper water under rocks, piles of driftwood, overhangs, and other objects. Feeds at night on fish, crayfish, aquatic insects, and other invertebrates. Males search out females in autumn and mate in depressions under large rocks, logs, boards, or other submerged objects. Female attaches eggs to underside of rocks or logs the following spring. Larvae hatch in 1–2 months and mature in 5–6 years.

Status: Statewide but seldom seen, except by fishermen. Probably more abundant and widespread prior to extensive stream modification.

Mudpuppy (*Necturus maculosus*), Vermilion Co., IL. (MR)

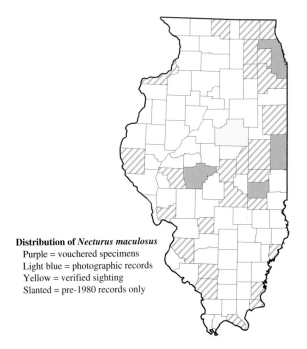

Distribution of *Necturus maculosus*
 Purple = vouchered specimens
 Light blue = photographic records
 Yellow = verified sighting
 Slanted = pre-1980 records only

Eastern newt   **Salamandridae**
Notophthalmus viridescens

Key Characters: No costal grooves or distinct gular fold; raised crests between eyes.

Similar Species: Recently transformed *Ambystoma*.

Subspecies: Central newt, *N. v. louisianensis*.

Description: Small (up to 11 cm TL), olive green to yellowish brown (reddish brown in efts) salamander, with small scattered black dots. Black-dotted yellow belly contrasts sharply with sides. Aquatic adult has tail fin. Breeding male has large hind legs with black ridges on thighs, black toe tips, and conspicuous pits behind eyes. Eft lacks tail fin, has more warty skin, and yellowish or reddish belly.

Habitat: Semi-permanent ponds and sloughs in or near forests.

Natural History: This salamander has an unusual three-part life history. Adults and larvae are aquatic, but there is an intermediate terrestrial stage called the eft. During spring, adult females attach tiny, pale eggs individually to underwater plants. Best breeding ponds are fish-free, but extensively vegetated borders of stocked lakes are satisfactory. Aquatic larvae transform mid- to late summer into efts, which, after living on land for 1–3 years around bark, logs, rocks, and damp leaves, mature and return to breeding pond. Efts often walk about during the day after rain. In some permanent fish-free ponds, larvae develop into gilled, otherwise-transformed adults. Outside breeding season, adults may remain in pond or wander on land nearby.

Status: Common in some southern counties where swamps and breeding ponds persist and wooded habitat for efts remains. Reduced in central and northern Illinois by deforestation and drainage of ponds and marshes.

Eastern newt (*Notophthalmus viridescens*), Cook Co., IL. (MR)

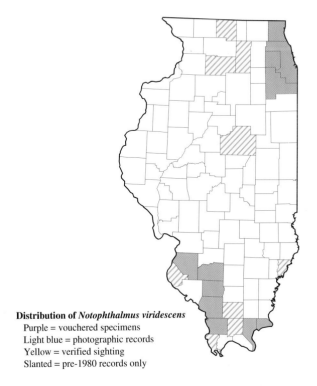

Distribution of *Notophthalmus viridescens*
  Purple = vouchered specimens
  Light blue = photographic records
  Yellow = verified sighting
  Slanted = pre-1980 records only

Lesser siren

Sirenidae

Siren intermedia

Key Characters: External gills; short front legs; no hind legs.

Similar Species: None.

Subspecies: Western lesser siren, *S. i. nettingi*.

Description: Named for mythological sea nymphs, sirens are long (up to 46 cm TL), slender brownish black or dark olive salamanders with small black spots and light spots. Belly lighter than back. Elongated body bears 34–37 costal grooves. Toothless jaws covered with dark, keratinized sheaths. Males and females indistinguishable externally. Larva differs from older individual by having more extensive tail fin and distinctive orange-red markings that include head stripe from gill to gill by way of snout, band across back of head, and stripe down middle of back.

Habitat: Aquatic and nocturnal inhabitants of swamps, ditches, lowland ponds, and sloughs.

Natural History: This permanently aquatic salamander burrows by day in debris and muck, but may remain active most of year. In seasonally dry bodies of water, they descend into burrows, produce a cocoon from skin gland secretions, and estivate until water returns. Adults eat worms, snails, and crayfish. Little is known about courtship and mating. Small larvae (about 24 mm TL) appear in May, grow quickly, and within a year some are 20 cm TL. Maturation probably requires 3–4 years. Underwater microphones have detected clicking sounds produced by sirens when they approach each other.

Status: Common in the southern quarter of the state and in places along the Illinois and Wabash rivers. May be even more widespread than thought, but infrequently seen because of secretive habits.

Lesser siren (*Siren intermedia*), Jackson Co., IL. (MR)

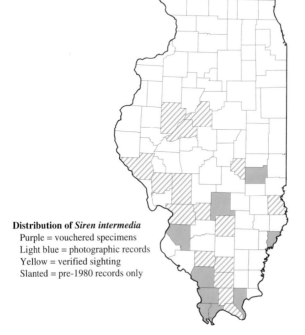

Distribution of *Siren intermedia*
Purple = vouchered specimens
Light blue = photographic records
Yellow = verified sighting
Slanted = pre-1980 records only

ORDER ANURA — FROGS & TOADS

Twenty-one species of frogs and toads representing five families occur in Illinois. Although usually secretive, these species may be the most conspicuous of the amphibians and reptiles in the state during the breeding season because of the loud vocalizations of the males. Also, frogs and toads have a unique body form. While salamanders may be confused with lizards, frogs and toads are unmistakable because of their short bodies, large heads, and enlarged hind legs. Like salamanders, most frogs and toads live in water or in cool, high-humidity environments in or near the ground. Also like salamanders, they lack scales and have a thin, respiratory skin covered with a layer of moisture secreted by glands. Because of their thicker skins, Illinois' two species of toad (family Bufonidae) can withstand slightly drier conditions than frogs. The treefrogs (family Hylidae) are distinctive in having adhesive disks (toe pads) at the ends of their toes (toe pads of some species are large, of others quite small). The true frogs (family Ranidae) probably are the most familiar members of the order Anura, and include the common leopard frogs and the bullfrog, which is the largest species in Illinois. Two families are represented in Illinois by only one species each. The eastern spadefoot (family Pelobatidae) and eastern narrowmouth (Microhylidae) often are called toads, but lack the extensive warts and cranial crests of true toads (family Bufonidae).

Most adult frogs and toads can be identified by presence or absence of toe pads, dorsolateral folds on the back, parotoid glands on the head, and the amount of webbing between toes. Tadpoles, however, present a challenge and are best identified by allowing them to transform and develop juvenile coloration.

The Illinois chorus frog has a limited distribution within the state and is restricted to sandy soils. Cricket frog populations appear to be declining in the northern third of the state. Many populations of other species have been eliminated, reduced, or fragmented through loss of habitat: draining of wetlands, channelization of streams, reduction of temporary ponds and sloughs, and clearing of forests (see "Declining Amphibian Populations," p. 12).

In species accounts, size is given as "cm SVL," the straight line length from the tip of the nose to the anal opening, in centimeters. Maximum size is the greatest recorded for a specimen from Illinois unless stated otherwise.

American toad
Bufo americanus

Bufonidae

Key Characters: Usually one or two large warts in each dark back spot; enlarged warts on lower leg; pronounced cranial crests.

Similar Species: Fowler's toad, eastern spadefoot.

Subspecies: Eastern American toad, *B. a. americanus*; dwarf American toad, *B. a. charlesmithi*.

Description: Large (up to 10 cm SVL) gray, brown, or reddish brown toad with numerous dark spots on back and heavily mottled chest and belly. Large bean-shaped parotoid gland behind each eye contacts cranial crests by short spur. Cranial crests higher than in Fowler's toad and more massive. The dwarf subspecies is much smaller and has less extensive mottling on chest and belly.

Habitat: Virtually all forest and prairie habitats in Illinois, including urban and agricultural areas, where flooded fields, ditches, and other bodies of water are available for reproduction.

Natural History: Outside of the breeding season, adults can be found under logs, rocks, and surface debris even in extremely dry microhabitats. Diet includes insects and earthworms. Poisonous skin secretions deter some predators. Breeding occurs from mid-April to early May when sustained high-pitched trills of males are heard from almost every aquatic habitat. Young males may call through late summer. Females lay several thousand black eggs in long strings held together by semitransparent membranes. Eggs hatch in a week and small jet-black tadpoles, which usually congregate in shallow water, transform within 40 days. Hundreds of tiny metamorphs are sometimes seen crossing nearby roads and trails.

Status: Common throughout state, except Wabash Border Division (Fig. 1). Known to hybridize with Fowler's toad in lower Mississippi River bottoms.

American toad (*Bufo americanus*), Will Co., IL. (MR)

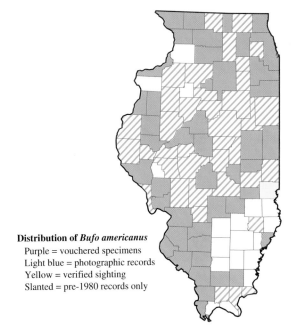

Distribution of *Bufo americanus*
  Purple = vouchered specimens
  Light blue = photographic records
  Yellow = verified sighting
  Slanted = pre-1980 records only

Fowler's toad
Bufo fowleri

Bufonidae

Key Characters: Three or more small warts in each dark back spot; warts on lower leg not noticeably enlarged; cranial crests low and less massive than American toad.

Similar Species: American toad, eastern spadefoot.

Subspecies: Sometimes considered a subspecies of Woodhouse's toad, *B. woodhousii fowleri*.

Description: Medium-sized (up to 8 cm SVL), gray to greenish gray toad with large dark back spots roughly in pairs flanking light midback stripe. Chest and belly white or gray; dark pigment, if any, limited to small spot on chest. Transverse cranial crest in broad contact with parotoid gland. Hybrids with *B. americanus* have intermediate features.

Habitat: A wide variety of habitats where flooded fields, ditches, and other bodies of water are available for reproduction.

Natural History: Adults are active on the surface day and night. Diet consists of insects, earthworms, and other invertebrates. Breeding takes place from late April to late June. The male breeding call, a short "waaaa," is heard from shallows of ponds and lakes and flooded ditches. Eggs are laid in long strings. Eggs and tadpoles are similar to those of American toad. Embryos hatch in a week and transform from June through July.

Status: Common in southern half of state and along Illinois and Mississippi rivers. Occasionally hybridizes with American toad in lower Mississippi River valley.

Fowler's toad (*Bufo fowleri*), Alexander Co., IL. (MR)

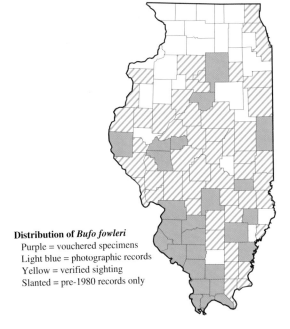

Distribution of *Bufo fowleri*
  Purple = vouchered specimens
  Light blue = photographic records
  Yellow = verified sighting
  Slanted = pre-1980 records only

Cricket frog
Acris crepitans

Hylidae

Key Characters: Warty skin; tiny toe pads; dark triangle between eyes.

Similar Species: Young western and upland chorus frogs.

Subspecies: Blanchard's cricket frog, *A. c. blanchardi*.

Description: Small (up to 3 cm SVL) olive brown frog with an elongate green or red stripe on back and a light line from eye to shoulder. Belly pale except for dark throat of male. Extensive webbing between toes of hind feet, dark stripe on posterior surface of thigh, and white wart on each side of cloacal opening.

Habitat: Shallow margins of lakes, ponds, marshes, and streams, where they are active even in very cold weather.

Natural History: This small frog commonly leaps into water when disturbed, then almost immediately swims back to shore. Adult diet includes small terrestrial insects and spiders. Breeds usually from late April to August. Male calls while floating on water or on mats of algae or duckweed and emits a series of sharp clicks, cricketlike or like the sound of striking marbles. Female lays masses of 10–15 tiny eggs (up to 200 eggs total), which hatch in a few days. Tadpole has black-tipped tail and transforms by mid-September.

Status: Once one of the most common frogs in the Midwest, but it has declined over much of northern Illinois. Threats are not well understood.

Cricket frog (*Acris crepitans*), Fayette Co., IL. (MR)

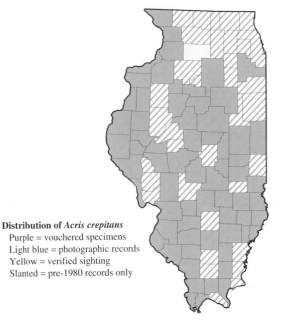

Distribution of *Acris crepitans*
Purple = vouchered specimens
Light blue = photographic records
Yellow = verified sighting
Slanted = pre-1980 records only

Bird-voiced treefrog   **Hylidae**
Hyla avivoca

Key Characters: Smooth skin; large toe pads; light spot under each eye; green to yellowish green patches in groin and inner thigh.

Similar Species: Gray treefrogs.

Description: Small (up to 3.5 cm SVL) gray-brown or greenish treefrog with dark "X" or star-shaped mark in middle of back. Belly pale; throat pouch dark in male. Arms and legs with dark bars. Eyes relatively large. Pustule underneath joint of outer finger of hand usually divided. Male smaller than female.

Habitat: Baldcypress-tupelo swamps and nearby wet hardwood forests.

Natural History: This small frog can change color from dark gray to light green depending on temperature, moisture, and background. Adult diet includes small arboreal insects and spiders. Breeds mid-May to August. Male calls from tree (often quite high up), vine, or large shrub over water, the sound a rapid succession of short birdlike whistles. Eggs are laid in submerged packets that hatch in a few days into colorful tadpoles (dark brown with 3–7 red saddles and thin bronze head stripes) that transform in about a month.

Status: Threatened in Illinois. Known only from extreme southern counties, where it is locally common in some good habitats. Threats include clearing and draining of baldcypress-tupelo swamps.

Bird-voiced treefrog (*Hyla avivoca*), Union Co., IL. (MR)

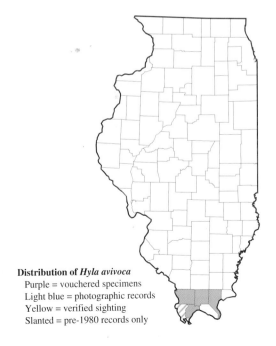

Distribution of *Hyla avivoca*
  Purple = vouchered specimens
  Light blue = photographic records
  Yellow = verified sighting
  Slanted = pre-1980 records only

Green treefrog
Hylidae

Hyla cinerea

Key Characters: Smooth skin; large toe pads; white or pale yellow stripe from upper lip to groin.

Similar Species: Gray treefrogs.

Description: Medium-sized (up to 6 cm SVL) bright green, yellowish green, olive green, or lime green frog with a few small splatters of gold or white. Belly clear pale yellow to white. Male slightly smaller than female. The male has a wrinkled throat indicating a vocal pouch.

Habitat: Open brushy borders of cypress swamps, floodplain sloughs, cattail marshes, lakes, and farm ponds.

Natural History: Adults and juveniles are seen on roads during and after rain. Diet consists of insects. Can change between dark and light green depending on temperature and lighting. Perches by day on upright cattail or other plant while legs are tightly tucked under body. Breeds late May to August. Males call, sometimes in large choruses, from button bush, swamp rose, lily pads, or other shoreline plants, and calls sound like a series of metallic honks, similar to cow bells or barking dogs. Eggs are laid under water surface and are attached to roots of floating vegetation. Embryos hatch in a few days and tadpoles transform in two months. Juveniles often feed in nearby grassy fields in late summer and autumn.

Status: Locally abundant in extreme southern counties where cypress and tupelo occur in dense stands. Has been introduced in a few areas north of its natural range.

Green treefrog (*Hyla cinerea*), Union Co., IL. (MR)

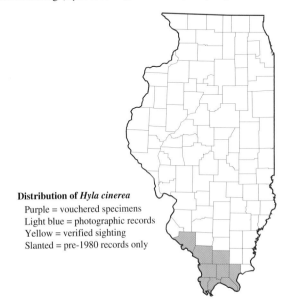

Distribution of *Hyla cinerea*
Purple = vouchered specimens
Light blue = photographic records
Yellow = verified sighting
Slanted = pre-1980 records only

Gray treefrogs

Hylidae

Hyla chrysoscelis & Hyla versicolor

Comment: Individuals of these two nearly identical species are distinguishable only by chromosome number (*H. chrysoscelis* is diploid, *H. versicolor* is tetraploid) and mating call (trill rate is faster in *H. chrysoscelis*).

Key Characters: Large toe pads; pale spot under eye; orange or golden yellow patches in groin and inner thigh.

Similar Species: Bird-voiced treefrog, green treefrog.

Description: Medium-sized (up to 6 cm SVL) brown or greenish brown frog with a black star-shaped or irregular X-shaped blotch on back. Belly pale, throat of male dark. Dark bars on arms and legs. Pustule under joint of outer finger of hand usually not divided. Recently transformed juvenile is bright green.

Habitat: Trunks and branches of trees. Adults mate in woodland pools, roadside ditches, and other temporary bodies of water.

Natural History: May change color from dark gray to light green depending on temperature and background. Diet consists of small insects and spiders. Feeding adults and juveniles are often attracted to house lights and windows where insects accumulate. Breeds late April to August. Breeding call is a guttural trill resembling Red-bellied Woodpecker song. Eggs, laid in packets attached to vegetation at water's surface, hatch in a few days and tadpoles transform in about two months. Bold red-orange and black tadpole tail provides easy identification.

Status: Common to very common throughout Illinois, but ranges of the two species remain to be distinguished.

Gray treefrog complex (*Hyla chrysoscelis-versicolor*), Union Co., IL. (MR)

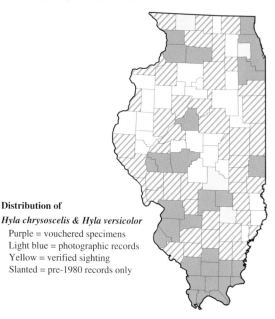

Distribution of

Hyla chrysoscelis & Hyla versicolor

Purple = vouchered specimens
Light blue = photographic records
Yellow = verified sighting
Slanted = pre-1980 records only

Spring peeper   **Hylidae**
Pseudacris crucifer

Key Characters: Large toe pads; dark "X" on back; dark spot or narrow bar between eyes.

Similar Species: Gray treefrogs, bird-voiced treefrog.

Description: Small (up to 3.5 cm SVL) tan, brown, or gray frog with dark diagonal lines suggesting an "X" on back. Belly white, sometimes with dark flecks. Snout projects beyond lower jaw when viewed in profile. No light spot under eye, or light stripe on upper jaw. Male with folded skin under throat indicating vocal pouch.

Habitat: Mesic forests, on trees, shrubs, and herbaceous plants. Most often seen around woodland pools in spring; seldom seen outside breeding season. Breeds in ponds and water-filled depressions in upland forest.

Natural History: Aptly named because it is one of first frogs to call each spring. Diet consists of small insects and spiders. Mates late February through May; some males call in autumn. Call is a soft, clear, ascending "peeeep" repeated about once each second and heard both day and night. Males commonly call in alternating duets or trios while perched in vegetation over water or on surface of water. Several hundred eggs per female, attached singly to sticks or leaf petioles, hatch in a few days, and tadpoles transform in about two months.

Status: Found throughout much of the state, especially along wooded floodplains and wooded uplands where it may be locally common.

Spring peeper (*Pseudacris crucifer*), Alexander Co., IL. (MR)

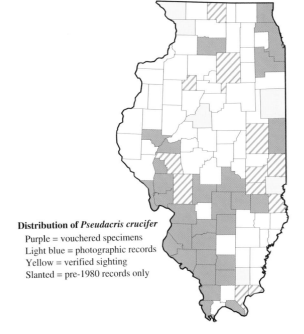

Distribution of *Pseudacris crucifer*
Purple = vouchered specimens
Light blue = photographic records
Yellow = verified sighting
Slanted = pre-1980 records only

Upland chorus frog

Hylidae

Pseudacris feriarum

Key Characters: Three thin, dark stripes, often broken into spots, on back; white stripe on upper jaw; toe pads small; no webbing between toes.

Similar Species: Western chorus frog, Strecker's chorus frog, spring peeper.

Subspecies: Upland chorus frog, *P. f. feriarum.*

Description: Small (up to 4 cm SVL) gray, tan, or brown frog with dark spots or stripes. Belly cream with scattered dark flecks. Middle section of leg (tibia) at least 47% as long as SVL. Distinct dark stripe on each side from snout through eye and along side to groin. Male smaller than female. Male with dark vocal pouch during breeding season.

Habitat: Forests, forest edges, and nearby open marshy fields. Breeds in nearly any shallow, temporary body of water, even a considerable distance from forest.

Natural History: To many people the calls of this frog and spring peepers are the symbols of spring. Diet consists of small arthropods. Mates late February through May, peaking in March. Males often chorus in large numbers while perched at edge of water or floating on it. Call is similar to sound produced by running finger down teeth of comb. Eggs (about 100 per female) are laid in elongate clusters attached to sticks or leaf petioles. Embryos hatch in a few days and tadpoles transform in about two months.

Status: One of the most common frogs throughout the extreme southern counties. Range may overlap slightly with western chorus frog.

Upland chorus frog (*Pseudacris feriarum*), Pope Co., IL. (MR)

Distribution of *Pseudacris feriarum*

Purple = vouchered specimens
Light blue = photographic records
Yellow = verified sighting
Slanted = pre-1980 records only

Strecker's chorus frog   **Hylidae**
Pseudacris streckeri

Key Characters: Stout toadlike body; no toe pads; robust forearms; dark masklike stripe from snout to shoulder; dark spot under eye; V- or Y-shaped mark between eyes.

Similar Species: Upland chorus frog, western chorus frog.

Subspecies: Illinois chorus frog, *P. s. illinoensis.*

Description: Small (up to 4.7 cm SVL) tan to gray frog with dark brown or black lines on back. Belly white. Skin granular rather than smooth. Throat (vocal pouch) of male dark during breeding season.

Habitat: Sand prairies and remnants such as sandy agricultural fields and waste areas. Burrows in sand and emerges after heavy, early spring rains to breed in nearby flooded fields, ditches, and other vernal ponds.

Natural History: Unusual because it digs forward with its stout front legs, rather than backward like the spadefoot and toads. Diet consists of small insects. Spends most of life underground, coming to surface during rain to breed for a few weeks during February–April. Breeding call is a series of clear high-pitched whistles. Eggs are laid in small, jelly-covered clusters attached to twigs and branches underwater. Embryos hatch in a few days and tadpoles transform in about two months.

Status: Threatened in Illinois. Locally abundant in undisturbed sand prairies in Cass and Morgan counties. Threats include drainage and cultivation of breeding ponds and adult habitat.

Strecker's chorus frog (*Pseudacris streckeri*), Alexander Co., IL. (MR)

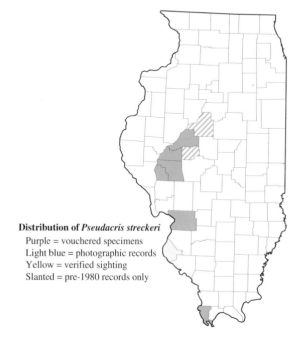

Distribution of *Pseudacris streckeri*

Purple = vouchered specimens
Light blue = photographic records
Yellow = verified sighting
Slanted = pre-1980 records only

Western chorus frog   **Hylidae**
Pseudacris triseriata

Key Characters: Three thin, dark stripes on back; white stripe on upper jaw; toe pads small; no webbing between toes.

Similar Species: Upland chorus frog, Strecker's chorus frog, spring peeper.

Description: Small (up to 4 cm SVL) gray, tan, or brown frog with black stripes. Belly cream with scattered dark flecks. Middle section of leg (tibia) less than 47% as long as SVL. Male smaller than female. Male has a dark vocal pouch during breeding season.

Habitat: Found in almost any type of wet habitat, including agricultural fields and urban settings, such as city parks, as long as vernal breeding pools are available. Breeds in ditches, flooded fields, floodplain depressions, even in wet areas along the busiest highways. Seldom seen outside the spring breeding season, so nonbreeding habitat is poorly known.

Natural History: Diet consists of small arthropods. Mates mid-February through May, often in large choruses. Call is similar to sound produced by running finger down teeth of comb, very similar to call of upland chorus frog. Eggs laid in small packets attached to sticks and leaf petioles. Embryos hatch in a few days and tadpoles transform is about two months.

Status: One of the most common spring frogs in the northern two-thirds of Illinois. Range may overlap slightly with upland chorus frog.

Western chorus frog (*Pseudacris triseriata*), DuPage Co., IL. (MR)

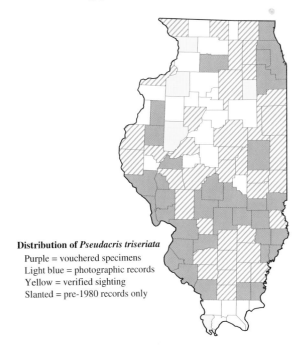

Distribution of *Pseudacris triseriata*

Purple = vouchered specimens
Light blue = photographic records
Yellow = verified sighting
Slanted = pre-1980 records only

Eastern narrowmouth toad   **Microhylidae**
Gastrophryne carolinensis

Key Characters: Squat body; narrow, pointed head; fold of skin across top of head behind eyes; no visible tympanum.

Similar Species: None.

Description: Small (up to 3.3 cm SVL) olive, dark gray, reddish brown, or nearly black frog with darkly mottled belly. Skin smooth, without warts or ridges. Legs stubby and toes without webbing or toe pads. Male has a dark throat.

Habitat: Open, moist areas with abundant ground cover. Breeds in temporary or permanent waters such as ponds, lakes, swamp edges, marshy fields, and roadside ditches.

Natural History: One of the few amphibians that feeds regularly on ants. Fold of skin on head is used to push ants away from eyes. Outside of breeding season it is found in rotten stumps and beneath rocks, logs, bark, and other objects on ground. Weak jumper, moves by short, rapid hops. Breeds in summer. Male usually calls from edge of water, concealed under plant debris. Call is a high-pitched buzz or "baaa" reminiscent of distressed lamb. When male amplexes female, sticky substance secreted from glands on his belly glues him temporarily to her back. Female lays over 800 tiny eggs in one layer at water surface. Embryos hatch in a few days and tadpoles transform in 20–70 days.

Status: Known from only six southern counties, where it may be locally common.

Eastern narrowmouth toad (*Gastrophryne carolinensis*), Monroe Co., IL. (MR)

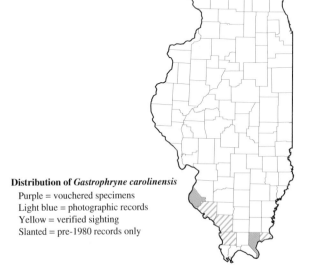

Distribution of *Gastrophryne carolinensis*
  Purple = vouchered specimens
  Light blue = photographic records
  Yellow = verified sighting
  Slanted = pre-1980 records only

Eastern spadefoot
Pelobatidae

Scaphiopus holbrookii

Key Characters: Plump body; vertical pupil; one large, black, elongate digging spade under heel of each hind foot.

Similar Species: American toad, Fowler's toad.

Subspecies: Eastern spadefoot, *S. h. holbrookii*.

Description: Medium-sized (up to 6 cm SVL) brown or yellow-brown frog, sometimes very dark. Pair of yellowish stripes usually extends from eye down back, converging in middle of back to outline an hourglass. Belly gray to white, without spots. Skin with small warts that may be tipped with red (especially in juveniles). Parotoid gland small, nearly round, and located above tympanum. Male smaller than female. Male has black horny coverings on first two fingers, and a conspicuous dark vocal pouch during breeding season.

Habitat: Forested and open areas, in sandy or loose soils. Breeds, often in large numbers, in temporary pools and flooded fields.

Natural History: An insectivorous species that spends much of life underground, where it burrows rearfirst using spades on hind feet. Nocturnal when above ground. Most often seen at breeding site, during field plowing, under logs and rocks, or on roads after heavy rain. Explosive breeder producing noisy choruses for brief periods following heavy rain from April to September. Breeding call is a series of low-pitched explosive groans. Reproduction adapted to ephemeral waters; eggs hatch in a few days and tadpoles transform in 2–3 weeks.

Status: Occurs in southern counties where, because of its secretive nature and burrowing habits, its abundance may be underestimated.

Eastern spadefoot (*Scaphiopus holbrookii*), Alexander Co., IL. (MR)

Distribution of *Scaphiopus holbrookii*

Purple = vouchered specimens
Light blue = photographic records
Yellow = verified sighting
Slanted = pre-1980 records only

Crawfish frog   **Ranidae**
Rana areolata

Key Characters: Large head; mottled upper jaws; distinctively humped lower back when at rest; dark spots on back crowded together and encircled by light borders.

Similar Species: Northern leopard frog, pickerel frog, plains leopard frog, southern leopard frog.

Subspecies: Northern crawfish frog, *R. a. circulosa.*

Description: Large (6.6–11 cm SVL) spotted frog with dorsolateral fold along each side of body. Entire belly unspotted white. Snout cone-shaped. Male has paired vocal pouches, at corners of jaw, and enlarged thumbs used for holding onto female during amplexus.

Habitat: Prairies, woodlands, and brushy fields in hardpan clay soils in low, wet areas. Common breeding sites include flooded fields, fish-free farm ponds, and small lakes in pastures or on golf courses.

Natural History: Lives underground most of year in mammal burrows, storm drains, and abandoned crayfish burrows. Known to eat crayfish and small amphibians and reptiles, mostly at burrow entrances. Adults breed in pools during March-April, sometimes in large numbers. Breeding call is a loud, deep snore. Female lays 3,000–7,000 eggs. Tadpoles transform in midsummer.

Status: Formerly widespread in southern half of state. Uncommon and declining in some areas where breeding habitats have been drained or stocked with predatory fishes.

Crawfish frog (*Rana areolata*), Williamson Co., IL. (MR)

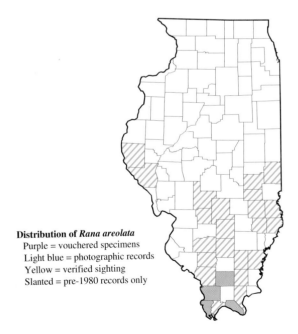

Distribution of *Rana areolata*
  Purple = vouchered specimens
  Light blue = photographic records
  Yellow = verified sighting
  Slanted = pre-1980 records only

Plains leopard frog
Ranidae

Rana blairi

Key Characters: Darkly spotted; dorsolateral folds along sides interrupted near posterior ends and offset toward midline.

Similar Species: Crawfish frog, northern leopard frog, pickerel frog, southern leopard frog.

Description: Medium-sized (5–9.5 cm TL) gray or brown leopard frog with rounded dark brown spots on back. Distinct light line extends along upper jaw from near snout tip to tympanum or slightly beyond. Light spot usually on tympanum, and dark spot on snout. Pale borders around back spots very narrow or absent. Belly white with greenish yellow near groin and underside of thigh. Chest and throat sometimes mottled.

Habitat: Uncultivated former prairies, marshlands, along creeks, in open bottomlands, and in old fields (former prairie) not far from water. Breeds in still waters of pools, roadside and drainage ditches, marshes, and ponds.

Natural History: In many places, occurs with the more abundant southern leopard frog, with which it occasionally hybridizes. In some places in northern parts of its range it occurs with northern leopard frog. Eats a variety of invertebrates. Adults breed during March–April, sometimes in large numbers. Breeding call is described as guttural "chuck-chuck-chuck." Female lays 3,000–7,000 eggs. Tadpoles transform in midsummer.

Status: Formerly widespread in extensive prairie marshlands of the state. Remains widespread, but not abundant, in peripheral prairie remnants and south along the Mississippi River bottomlands. Most of original habitat has been rendered unsuitable by agriculture.

Plains leopard frog (*Rana blairi*), Jackson Co., IL. (MR)

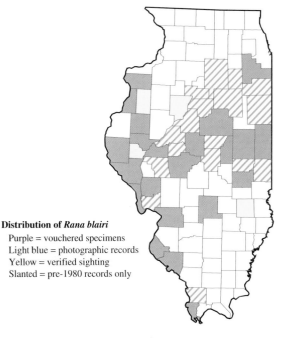

Distribution of *Rana blairi*
  Purple = vouchered specimens
  Light blue = photographic records
  Yellow = verified sighting
  Slanted = pre-1980 records only

Bullfrog   **Ranidae**
Rana catesbeiana

Key Characters: Well-developed dorsolateral folds tracing rear border of tympanum but not extending onto sides of body; toes webbed nearly to tips.

Similar Species: Green frog.

Description: Large (9–15 cm SVL) olive, green, or brown frog sometimes with dots or obscure black blotches on back. Backs of juveniles and tadpoles covered with small, evenly scattered black dots. Belly ranges from white to yellow, in some individuals marked with black spots or networks. Tympanum distinctly larger than eye. Males with single vocal pouch under lower jaw, yellow throat, larger tympanum and, during the breeding season, swollen thumbs.

Habitat: Permanent bodies of water (lakes, ponds, rivers, sluggish portions of streams) in forests, prairies, and disturbed habitats (including urban areas).

Natural History: Adult tends to be solitary. Eats any animal it can capture and swallow: arthropods, other frogs, snakes, even small mammals and birds. Bullfrogs have been introduced as food for humans in some parts of the world. Breeding male emits deep bass "jug-a-rum" breeding call. During long summer breeding season (April–August), males sometimes aggressively defend part of pond and mate with entering females. Thousands of eggs are laid in summer. Tadpoles overwinter and transform the following summer.

Status: Abundant statewide in permanent aquatic habitats.

Bullfrog (*Rana catesbeiana*), Jackson Co., IL. (MR)

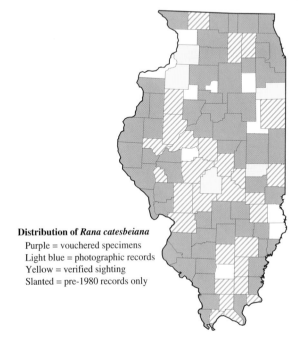

Distribution of *Rana catesbeiana*
 Purple = vouchered specimens
 Light blue = photographic records
 Yellow = verified sighting
 Slanted = pre-1980 records only

Green frog
Rana clamitans

Ranidae

Key Characters: Well-developed fold around rear of tympanum extends middle way down the back; toes webbed about halfway to tips.

Similar Species: Bullfrog.

Subspecies: Green frog, *R. c. melanota*; and intergrades between the green frog and the bronze frog, *R. c. clamitans*.

Description: Medium-sized (5.7–9.5 cm TL) olive, brown, or green frog with dim black spots on back. Chin, breast, and undersides of legs sometimes marked with dark spots or mottling. Mature male with larger tympanum, enlarged thumbs during breeding season, stouter front legs, bright green upper jaw, and yellow throat. In southwestern counties, males tend to have dusky upper jaws and green throats.

Habitat: A variety of shallow, weedy, aquatic habitats around lakes, ponds, and streams in wooded areas. In southern counties, where rock outcrops are abundant, it often is associated with small spring-fed streams.

Natural History: Like bullfrogs and leopard frogs, startled individuals emit loud, high-pitched yelps as they jump. Breeding calls (1–3 explosive banjolike twangs) are heard from May to September. Paired vocal pouches are not evident externally. Tadpoles overwinter to transform the following summer.

Status: Abundant in northern Illinois, the Shawnee Hills, parts of eastern Illinois, and along Middle Mississippi Border Division (Fig. 1). Absent from Grand Prairie and most of Southern Till Plain counties.

Green frog (*Rana clamitans*), DuPage Co., IL. (MR)

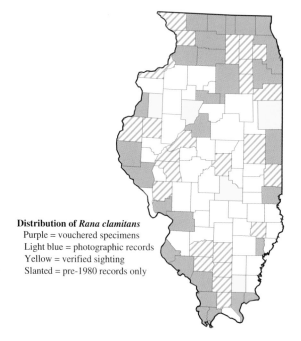

Distribution of *Rana clamitans*
  Purple = vouchered specimens
  Light blue = photographic records
  Yellow = verified sighting
  Slanted = pre-1980 records only

Pickerel frog   **Ranidae**
Rana palustris

Key Characters: Two rows of somewhat square black spots on back between wide dorsolateral folds that extend from eyes to hips; undersides of thighs bright yellow in life.

Similar Species: Crawfish frog, northern leopard frog, plains leopard frog, southern leopard frog.

Description: Small to medium-sized (4.5–7.0 cm SVL) gray or tan frog with back spots symmetrically arranged and square rather than round. Occasionally, spots fuse to form rectangles or long bars on back. On sides, spots are higher than long and aligned in one row. Belly plain white.

Habitat: Dense herbaceous vegetation along streams and within fens, often near forests. Rocky, spring-fed streams along Middle Mississippi Border Division (Fig. 1). Characteristic animal of cave entranceways.

Natural History: Lives in cool, high-quality waters, and can withstand lower temperature than most other species of *Rana*. Adults migrate to clear, cool ponds to mate during April–May and females lay about 2,000 eggs each. Breeding call is a low, snoring sound lasting 1–2 seconds. Tadpoles transform by midsummer.

Status: Uncommon, vulnerable to habitat deterioration. A habitat specialist, its distribution is fragmentary and incompletely known.

Pickerel frog (*Rana palustris*), Randolph Co., IL. (MR)

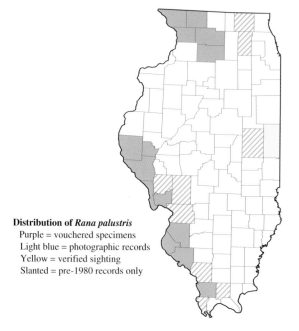

Distribution of *Rana palustris*
  Purple = vouchered specimens
  Light blue = photographic records
  Yellow = verified sighting
  Slanted = pre-1980 records only

Northern leopard frog   **Ranidae**
Rana pipiens

Key Characters: Dark spots on back rounded, white margined, and mostly larger than eye; most individuals with dark spot on snout and unspotted tympanum.

Similar Species: Crawfish frog, pickerel frog, plains leopard frog, southern leopard frog.

Description: Medium-sized (5–9.6 cm SVL) green, tan, or brown frog with white belly and undersides of legs. Pale dorsolateral fold from each eye along back; often, additional but less prominent ridges between them. As in other leopard frogs and pickerel frogs, but not crawfish frogs, a light line runs along upper jaw. Vocal pouches at angles of jaws visible when male calls.

Habitat: Streams, ponds, lakes, wet prairies, and other bodies of water, frequently moving into grassy, herbaceous fields or forest borders some distance from permanent water.

Natural History: This strong jumper is difficult to capture during day. Emits startling "warning screams" when jumping into water and, when grabbed, may release urine to discourage potential predator and reduce weight for jumping. Eats a variety of invertebrates. Winter is spent under submerged logs or rocks in small streams or marshes where large numbers may congregate. Breeding call is described as long, deep rattling snore interspersed with clucking grunts. Eggs are laid during March-May and tadpoles transform late June to August.

Status: Widespread in northern third of state. Local abundance varies year to year.

Northern leopard frog (*Rana pipiens*), DuPage Co., IL. (MR)

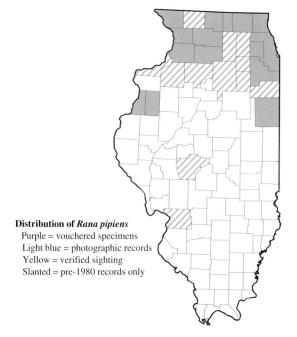

Distribution of *Rana pipiens*
  Purple = vouchered specimens
  Light blue = photographic records
  Yellow = verified sighting
  Slanted = pre-1980 records only

Southern leopard frog   **Ranidae**
Rana sphenocephala

Key Characters: Dark spots on back rounded; most individuals with light spot on tympanum; few dark spots on sides; no dark spot on snout; long, pointed head.

Similar Species: Crawfish frog, pickerel frog, northern leopard frog, plains leopard frog.

Description: Medium-sized (5–9 cm SVL) light tan, green, brown, or mixed green and brown frog. Belly and undersides of legs white in life. Continuous pale dorsolateral fold, narrower and whiter than in northern leopard frogs, extends from each eye along back. Back spots, sometimes fused together, rarely have white margins and are mostly smaller than eye. As in other leopard frogs and pickerel frogs, but not crawfish frogs, there is a light line on upper jaw. External vocal pouches of males usually visible at corners of jaws.

Habitat: This is a species of broad ecological tolerance and is found in all sorts of shallow water habitats. In summer, individuals venture away from shorelines and into nearby weed-and-grass-covered fields where they feed.

Natural History: Similar in habits to northern leopard frog. During the late February to mid-April breeding season, male produces breeding calls that sound like a mixed series of chuckles and groans. Female lays 1,000 to 4,000 eggs, and tadpoles transform by late spring/summer. May breed in autumn in southern counties.

Status: Widespread and locally abundant over southern half of state.

Southern leopard frog (*Rana sphenocephala*), Monroe Co., IL. (MR)

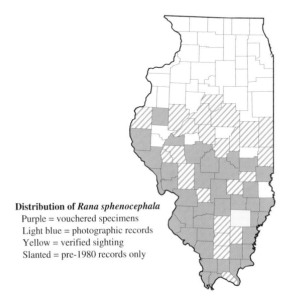

Distribution of *Rana sphenocephala*
Purple = vouchered specimens
Light blue = photographic records
Yellow = verified sighting
Slanted = pre-1980 records only

Wood frog   **Ranidae**
Rana sylvatica

Key Characters: Dark mask on side of face that obscures lower half of eye; dorsolateral fold extends from eye to hip; tympanum smaller than eye; 2–3 joints of the 4th toe free of webbing.

Similar Species: Green frog.

Description: Small to medium-sized (3.5–6.0 cm SVL) tan to reddish brown frog. Back occasionally sports a few scattered black dots. Legs sometimes crossed with dark bands. Breeding male is smaller than female, is darker, and has enlarged thumbs.

Habitat: Solitary inhabitant of mature, moist forests. May wander far from breeding habitats of shallow vernal pools and forest ponds.

Natural History: Well camouflaged to move about on forest floors, feeding and making long, low leaps when disturbed. Diet includes a variety of invertebrates. Large breeding aggregations appear in ponds and vernal forest pools after first warm rains of spring (mid-February to March in south, mid-March to April in north). The 5–6 clucking sounds of individual mating calls do not carry far. Female lays 300–900 eggs that hatch in 10 days to two weeks. Tadpoles grow rapidly and transform in May in the south, June in the north.

Status: Populations scattered in northern corners of state, in the east, and in Shawnee Hills, avoiding the Grand Prairie and Till Plains (Fig. 1). Localized populations more vulnerable than those of many frogs.

Wood frog (*Rana sylvatica*), Jackson Co., IL. (MR)

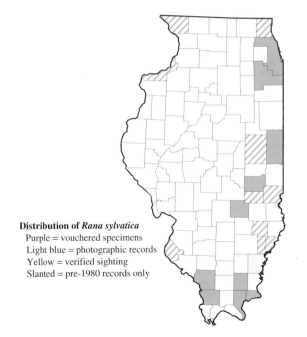

Distribution of *Rana sylvatica*
Purple = vouchered specimens
Light blue = photographic records
Yellow = verified sighting
Slanted = pre-1980 records only

ORDER TESTUDINES — TURTLES

Turtles are among the most distinctive reptiles. Salamanders can be confused with lizards, and legless lizards can be confused with snakes, but the unique shell identifies a turtle beyond doubt. Turtles dwell in forests, prairies, marshes, swamps, ponds, lakes, streams, and rivers. Because of their penchant for basking, many species are conspicuous on sunny days as they line almost every log and sand bank within the habitat. In the spring, turtles are also regularly encountered crossing highways as they search for new habitats, mates, or nesting sites. All species of turtle in Illinois bury their eggs in the soil. Seventeen species representing four families inhabit the state. The majority (11 species) are pond and box turtles (family Emydidae) while the mud turtles (family Kinosternidae) have three species, and the snapping turtles (family Chelydridae) and softshell turtles (family Trionychidae) contain two species each.

Fortunately, most adult turtles can be identified by their shell alone because newly captured animals typically retract their soft parts (i.e., head, neck, legs, and tail) within the shell making viewing difficult. Useful shell characteristics include a covering of scutes (large horny scales) or leathery skin, a hinged or solid plastron, and the number of plastral and marginal scutes. Should examination of the soft parts be necessary, a stubborn turtle can sometimes be coaxed into extending its head and neck by submergence in water or by picking it up by the rear edge of the shell so that the head hangs downward.

A number of turtles are of conservation concern. The yellow mud turtle, river cooter, alligator snapping turtle, and spotted turtle are state listed as endangered and Blanding's turtle as threatened. Furthermore, many of the other species are declining. A variety of causes may be cited but most are closely tied to human activity. Most problems either result directly from purposeful exploitation by humans or indirectly from habitat alteration. Direct causes include exploitation for food (usually snappers and softshells) and for the pet trade. Untold numbers are killed by automobiles as they attempt to cross highways.

Many are drowned in fishing nets set below the surface or are killed when they are caught on fishermen's hooks. Others are killed by irresponsible riflemen who inexplicably require living organisms for target practice. Indirect causes include draining of wetlands, pollution and siltation of aquatic habitats, and straightening of streams and rivers.

In the species accounts that follow, size is given in "cm CL," which is the straight line length of the carapace (upper shell) given in centimeters. The maximum size listed in the "Key Characters" section for each species is the greatest CL recorded for specimens in Illinois unless otherwise stated.

Snapping turtle
Chelydra serpentina

Chelydridae

Key Characters: Long neck; long tail with sawtooth projections on upper surface; carapace strongly serrate posteriorly, with three low keels (disappear with age) and one row of marginal scutes.

Similar Species: Alligator snapping turtle.

Subspecies: Common snapping turtle, *C. s. serpentina.*

Description: Large (up to 49 cm CL), aggressive, aquatic turtle with a relatively unpatterned carapace in cryptic shades of brown, olive, gray, or black. Head moderately large, beak moderately hooked, two chin barbels. Liberal covering of tubercles on back of neck. Plastron much reduced, cross-shaped, offering little protection. Legs muscular, feet broad with long claws and extensive webbing between toes. Male grows larger, has thicker tail base, and vent opening behind edge of carapace.

Habitat: Almost any body of water. Shallow, mud-bottomed backwaters and ponds with lush aquatic vegetation are especially favorable.

Natural History: Aggressive and menacing when encountered on land, but calm and retiring in water, where it seeks only escape when approached by humans; thus, it is little threat to swimmers. Although chiefly aquatic, it is often found away from water during spring. Eats a variety of invertebrates, vertebrates, and plants. Female lays one clutch of 20–40 spherical, leathery-shelled eggs (ca. 25–27 mm diameter) from mid-May to mid-June.

Status: Common statewide in habitats not used by fishermen. Although heavily exploited for human food, populations appear not to be threatened at this time.

Snapping turtle (*Chelydra serpentina*), Union Co., IL. (EOM)

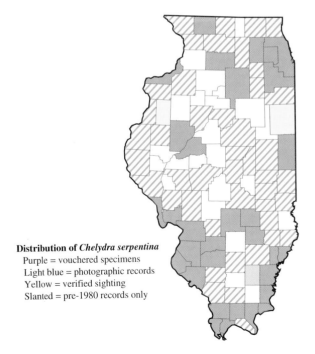

Distribution of *Chelydra serpentina*
Purple = vouchered specimens
Light blue = photographic records
Yellow = verified sighting
Slanted = pre-1980 records only

Alligator snapping turtle   **Chelydridae**
Macroclemys temminckii

Key Characters: Wormlike lure on tongue; three prominent keels on upper shell; extra set of marginals (= supramarginals) separates true marginals 4–7 from pleural scutes.

Similar Species: Common snapping turtle.

Description: Largest freshwater turtle in North America (record is 80 cm CL). Wild individuals rarely reach 70 kg (155 lb), but captives may exceed 100 kg (220 lb). Carapace sculptured, dull black or brown, and strongly serrate posteriorly. Three carapacial keels formed by pyramid-shaped elevations of vertebral and pleural scutes. Plastron reduced and cross-shaped. Head cannot be retracted within shell. Chin, throat, and neck decked with long, pointed tubercles. Tail nearly as long as shell. Male larger than female. Male cloacal opening extends about twice as far beyond back edge of shell (mean = 19.9 cm).

Habitat: Chiefly riverine, but also oxbow lakes, cypress swamps, and canals.

Natural History: Wormlike projection on floor of mouth effectively lures fish within range of jaws. Eats almost anything it can catch, including other turtles. Its eggs and young are eaten by variety of predators including raccoons, skunks, otters, and fish. Humans are chief predator of large adults. Large female captured in Union County in late June contained 32 spherical eggs, the largest of which was 35 mm diameter. Gaping jaws and strongly hooked beak of enraged adult are efficient deterrents to most potential predators.

Status: State endangered. Usually killed and eaten or displayed as oddity when found.

Alligator snapping turtle (*Macroclemys temminckii*), pet trade. (SB)

Distribution of *Macroclemys temminckii*
 Purple = vouchered specimens
 Light blue = photographic records
 Yellow = verified sighting
 Slanted = pre-1980 records only

Painted turtle   **Emydidae**
Chrysemys picta

Key Characters: Relatively low, smooth-edged shell; red markings on marginals or plastron; upper jaw with median notch bordered by toothlike cusps.

Similar Species: Slider (melanistic males).

Subspecies: Western painted turtle, *C. p. bellii*; midland painted turtle, *C. p. marginata*; and intergradation between midland and southern painted turtle, *C. p. dorsalis*.

Description: Medium-sized (up to 18 cm CL) turtle with yellow stripes on head and olive to black carapace. Marginal scutes with vertical bars (*bellii*) or horizontal to curved markings (*marginata*); red midback stripe broad (*dorsalis*), narrow (*marginata*), or absent (*bellii*). Plastron: yellow, red, or orange; dark markings broad, laterally branching, and covering most of plastron (*bellii*); elongated and confined to midplastral seam (*marginata*); or absent (*dorsalis*). Extensive intergradation among subspecies produces great variation within state.

Habitat: Frequents most aquatic habitats but most common in shallow, quiet, weedy parts of lakes, ponds, marshes, and river backwaters.

Natural History: Basking congregations are common on logs and banks. Omnivorous diet includes plants, insects, and mollusks. Readily scavenges on dead fish. Nests May to July. Lays 2–3 clutches of 8–9 flexible-shelled, ellipsoidal eggs (ca. 32 x 20 mm). Hatchlings usually overwinter in nest.

Status: Common and widespread. Highly adaptable, less susceptible to habitat modification than many turtles. Some collected illegally as pets, but no population appears seriously reduced.

Painted turtle (*Chrysemys picta*), DuPage Co., IL. (MR)

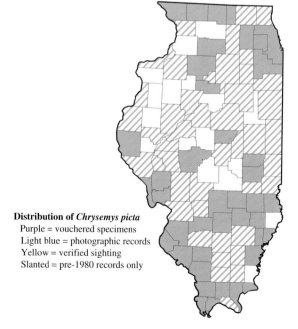

Distribution of *Chrysemys picta*
 Purple = vouchered specimens
 Light blue = photographic records
 Yellow = verified sighting
 Slanted = pre-1980 records only

Spotted turtle   **Emydidae**
Clemmys guttata

Key Characters: Unhinged plastron; low, smooth-margined, black carapace usually with one to several yellow spots per scute.

Similar Species: Juvenile Blanding's turtle.

Description: Small (up to 12 cm CL) distinctive turtle with a plastral pattern of dark blotches on light background that becomes darker with age. Head spotted or uniformly dark. Limbs dark above, yellow to orange below. Male usually with tan chin, brown eyes, and slightly concave plastron. Female with yellow chin, orange eyes, and flat plastron.

Habitat: Shallow wetlands including sedge meadows adjoining cattail marshes, and wet dolomite prairies.

Natural History: Cryptic, most noticeable when basking on muskrat lodges or clumps of sedge or cattails. Semiaquatic, moves moderate distances overland between wet areas. Diet includes crayfish, aquatic isopods, and insects. Three to five ellipsoidal eggs (ca. 31 x 18 mm) are laid in one clutch from May to July.

Status: State endangered. Historically known only from northeastern counties. Presently, extant populations only in Will County.

Spotted turtle (*Clemmys guttata*), Will Co., IL. (MR)

Distribution of *Clemmys guttata*
  Purple = vouchered specimens
  Light blue = photographic records
  Yellow = verified sighting
  Slanted = pre-1980 records only

Blanding's turtle   **Emydidae**
Emydoidea blandingii

Key Characters: Bright yellow chin and throat; notched upper jaw; hinged plastron.

Similar species: Box turtles, spotted turtle.

Description: Medium-sized (up to 24 cm CL) turtle with dark shell. Head and carapace profusely decked with light spots and dashes. Each plastral scute patterned with a large dark blotch usually bordered with yellow but, in older individuals, entire plastron may be black. Pleural scutes of young unpatterned or have faint radiating streaks. Disproportionately longer tail than box turtles. Male with concave plastron, heavier tail with cloacal opening behind edge of carapace, and dark markings on upper mandible.

Habitat: Quiet waters in marshes, prairie wetlands, wet sedge meadows, and shallow, vegetated portions of lakes.

Natural History: Usually found in and around water, but moves long distances overland. Long-lived, up to 77 years. Chiefly carnivorous, eating snails, insects, crayfish, and vertebrates. Female nests in late May and June, laying one clutch of about 12 hard-shelled, ellipsoidal eggs (ca. 30 x 20 mm).

Status: State threatened. Relatively common in appropriate habitat from Illinois River northward. Rare farther south. Major threat has been habitat destruction.

Blanding's turtle (*Emydoidea blandingii*), Cook Co., IL. (MR)

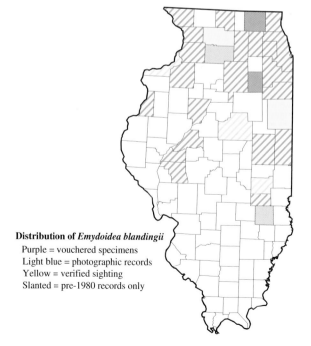

Distribution of *Emydoidea blandingii*

Purple = vouchered specimens
Light blue = photographic records
Yellow = verified sighting
Slanted = pre-1980 records only

Common map turtle   **Emydidae**
Graptemys geographica

Key Characters: Small, isolated, somewhat triangular spot or mark behind eye; carapace with sawtooth rear margin and low midback keel; vertebral knobs or spines distinct in juveniles, small in adult males, usually lost in old females.

Similar Species: False map turtle, Ouachita map turtle.

Description: Medium-sized (up to 24 cm CL) turtle. Carapace olive brown with network of yellow lines (resembling a road map); some lines encircle dark brown smudges. Vertebral knobs and keel dark brown. Plastron pale yellow with dark pigment bordering scute seams. Female larger than male and with broader head. Male with elongate foreclaws and cloacal opening behind end of carapace.

Habitat: Slow-moving stretches and backwaters of rivers as well as large lakes.

Natural History: Basks and dives into water at the slightest disturbance. Eats snails, clams, crayfish, and insects, which it crushes with broad surfaces of jaws. Female lays 2–3 clutches of about 12 ellipsoidal, leathery-shelled eggs (ca. 35 x 22 mm) between late May and early July and buries them in soft soil or sand.

Status: Most abundant in northern half of state. Locks and dams and dredging of upper Mississippi River have created excellent habitat pools dotted with sand bars.

Common map turtle (*Graptemys geographica*), Jo Daviess Co., IL. (EOM)
(Inset) Kentucky. (MR)

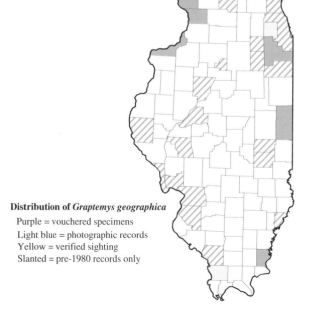

Distribution of *Graptemys geographica*

Purple = vouchered specimens
Light blue = photographic records
Yellow = verified sighting
Slanted = pre-1980 records only

Ouachita map turtle
Emydidae

Graptemys ouachitensis

Key Characters: Broad, yellow, vertical bar behind eye; large yellow spot under eye and on lower jaw; low knob-bearing keel along midline of back.

Similar Species: Common map turtle, false map turtle.

Subspecies: Ouachita map turtle, *G. o. ouachitensis.*

Description: Medium-sized (up to 22 cm CL) turtle. Carapace brown to olive, with black or dark brown knobs, and with dark blotches on posterior portion of each scute. In some individuals, blotches are encircled by yellow or orange lines; in others lines are present without blotches. Plastron yellowish and, in juveniles, patterned with dark swirls that cover up to half the plastral area. Plastral pattern obscure in old adults. Head, neck, limbs, and tail striped. Male with elongate foreclaws and vent behind end of carapace.

Habitat: Rivers with sand or gravel bottoms.

Natural History: Regularly basks in large numbers on logs and snags near river banks. Omnivorous, eats aquatic insect larvae and vegetation. Nesting occurs mid-May to early June. Two clutches of ellipsoidal, flexible-shelled eggs (ca. 19/clutch) are laid annually. Eggs average 35 x 22 mm.

Status: Locally common, particularly in Wabash River. Status and distribution poorly understood because of identification problems and confusion in literature.

Ouachita map turtle (*Graptemys ouachitensis*), Jackson Co., IL. (MR)

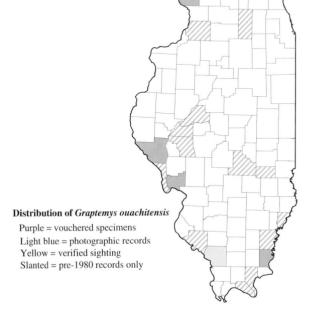

Distribution of *Graptemys ouachitensis*

Purple = vouchered specimens
Light blue = photographic records
Yellow = verified sighting
Slanted = pre-1980 records only

False map turtle
Graptemys pseudogeographica

Emydidae

Key Characters: Narrow vertical bar behind eye (sometimes forming semicircle); no large spot below eye or on lower jaw; low knob-bearing keel along midline of back.

Similar Species: Common map turtle, Ouachita map turtle.

Subspecies: False map turtle, *G. p. pseudogeographica*, and intergradation between false map turtle and Mississippi map turtle, *G. p. kohnii*.

Description: Medium-sized (up to 25 cm CL) turtle. Carapace brown to olive, with black or dark brown knobs. Posterior edge strongly toothed in young. Hatchling with orange or yellow rings on lateral carapace scutes and intricately whorled dark lines on plastron that fade to obscurity in adult. Head, neck, limbs, and tail liberally striped. Male with elongate foreclaws and cloacal opening behind end of carapace.

Habitat: Rivers and backwaters with mud bottoms and abundant basking sites.

Natural History: Extremely wary when basking, among first to dive into water when approached by boat. Omnivorous, feeding almost equally on plants and animals (mollusks and insects). Nests late May into early July. Female lays 2–3 clutches of ellipsoidal, flexible-shelled eggs (ca. 14/clutch).

Status: Locally common along Mississippi and Illinois rivers. Often confused with Ouachita map turtle in the literature. The Cook County populations may be introduced.

False map turtle (*Graptemys pseudogeographica*),
Alexander Co., IL. (MR)

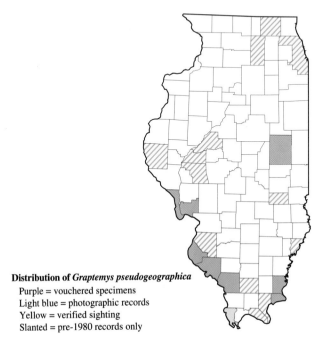

Distribution of *Graptemys pseudogeographica*

Purple = vouchered specimens
Light blue = photographic records
Yellow = verified sighting
Slanted = pre-1980 records only

River cooter
Pseudemys concinna

Emydidae

Key Characteristics: Intricately patterned carapace; unpatterned or sparsely patterned plastron; no red head stripe; no dark smudges on plastral scutes.

Similar Species: Slider.

Subspecies: Two interpretations exist. In one, all Illinois populations are the eastern river cooter, *P. c. concinna*. In the other, Ohio River and Wabash River populations are hieroglyphic sliders, *P. c. hieroglyphica*, and Mississippi River populations are intergrades between *P. c. hieroglyphica* and Missouri slider, *P. c. metteri*.

Description: Large (up to 32 cm CL) turtle with striped head. Adult carapace olive to dark brown, patterned with yellow or orange lines or swirls, flared posteriorly, and without keel along the back. Male with elongate foreclaws and vent behind end of carapace.

Habitat: Backwaters and oxbow lakes of large rivers and reservoirs.

Natural History: Basks regularly, but wary and difficult to approach. Young are omnivorous, adults are chiefly herbivorous. Courting male swims with and above female, vibrating foreclaws in her face. Female digs nest in soil during late spring and lays up to 20 ellipsoidal eggs (ca. 35 x 25 mm), usually more than once annually. Hatchlings emerge August–September, or overwinter in nest.

Status: State endangered. Populations persist along lower Wabash and Ohio rivers. Threats include pollution, drainage of backwaters, and flood control projects that isolate backwaters from rivers.

River cooter (*Pseudemys concinna*), Kentucky. (MR)

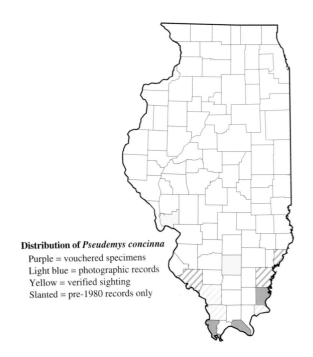

Distribution of *Pseudemys concinna*

Purple = vouchered specimens
Light blue = photographic records
Yellow = verified sighting
Slanted = pre-1980 records only

Eastern box turtle   **Emydidae**
Terrapene carolina

Key Characteristics: Keeled, high-domed carapace; hinged plastron lacking discrete pattern of light lines.

Similar Species: Ornate box turtle, Blanding's turtle.

Subspecies: Eastern box turtle, *T. c. carolina.*

Description: Small (up to 15 cm CL) turtle with highly variable carapace pattern of yellow or orange markings on dark background. Plastron tan or brown. Well-developed plastral hinge separates pectoral and abdominal scutes and allows shell to be closed completely. Male differs from female by having concave plastron and red rather than brown eyes. Carapace of hatchling round, brown, with pronounced keel and one yellow spot on each pleural and vertebral scute; plastron with dark central figure bordered by yellow.

Habitat: Forests and forest edges.

Natural History: Forages for berries, fungi, and a variety of invertebrates (earthworms, snails, slugs, insects). Two clutches of 3–8 ellipsoidal eggs (ca. 33 x 20 mm) are usually laid in June. Hibernates in late October or early November by burrowing into loose soil or pond bottom.

Status: Regularly seen in intact forests of southern half of state. Introduced by humans in urban areas throughout the state.

Eastern box turtle (*Terrapene carolina*), Williamson Co., IL. (MR)

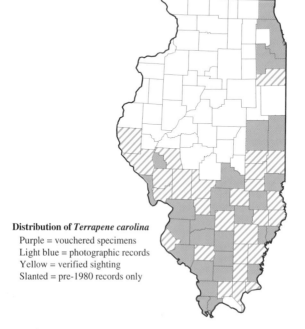

Distribution of *Terrapene carolina*
  Purple = vouchered specimens
  Light blue = photographic records
  Yellow = verified sighting
  Slanted = pre-1980 records only

Ornate box turtle   **Emydidae**
Terrapene ornata

Key Characteristics: Moderately high carapace flattened along midline and without keel; hinged plastron patterned with lines radiating from center of each scute.

Similar Species: Eastern box turtle, Blanding's turtle.

Subspecies: Ornate box turtle, *T. o. ornata*.

Description: Small (up to 13 cm CL) turtle with dark brown carapace, yellow midback stripe and yellow lines radiating from center of each scute (6–8 lines per pleural scute). Plastron patterned with yellow lines on dark scutes. Head sometimes spotted. Male differs from female by having slightly concave plastron and red rather than brown eyes. Hatchling resembles adult, but yellow markings are more like spots than lines.

Habitat: Prairies (other than black muck prairie) and open fields in former prairie.

Natural History: Tends to be more carnivorous than eastern box turtle, but eats some vegetation. Eats mainly insects, but also snails, earthworms, tadpoles, bird eggs and hatchlings, and carrion. Female lays one or more clutches of 4–6 ellipsoidal, relatively hard-shelled eggs (ca. 35 x 20 mm) in June. Hibernates about two weeks earlier than eastern box turtle, and emerges in spring about two weeks later.

Status: Uncommon to rare in much of its range in Illinois.

Ornate box turtle (*Terrapene ornata*), Washington Co., IL. (MR)

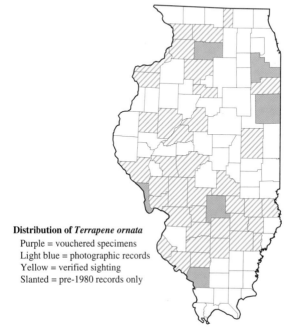

Distribution of *Terrapene ornata*
  Purple = vouchered specimens
  Light blue = photographic records
  Yellow = verified sighting
  Slanted = pre-1980 records only

Slider   **Emydidae**
Trachemys scripta

Key Characteristics: Bright red stripe behind eye; dark spot on each plastral scute.

Similar Species: River cooter.

Subspecies: Red-eared slider, *T. s. elegans.*

Description: Medium-sized (up to 26 cm CL) turtle with olive or green carapace. Vertical yellow bar through each lateral scute and additional yellow and dark lines parallel to each bar. Carapace low, with weak midback keel and serrate posterior edge. Keel and toothed edge of carapace disappear with age. Plastron yellow with dark markings. Old adults (particularly males) melanistic, with obscured pattern. Male with elongate foreclaws and vent opening beyond end of carapace.

Habitat: Most permanent bodies of water. Common in mud-bottomed sites rich in vegetation and basking structures.

Natural History: Omnivorous, feeds heavily on animal prey when young and becomes more herbivorous with maturation. Nests mid-May into early July. Female lays 5–18 ellipsoidal (ca. 36 x 22 mm) eggs per nest 2–3 times annually. Embryos hatch in two months.

Status: Adaptable and exceedingly common in Illinois.

Slider (*Trachemys scripta*), Union Co., IL. (EOM)

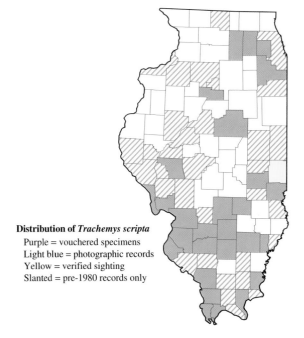

Distribution of *Trachemys scripta*
Purple = vouchered specimens
Light blue = photographic records
Yellow = verified sighting
Slanted = pre-1980 records only

Yellow mud turtle   **Kinosternidae**
Kinosternon flavescens

Key Characteristics: Peaked ninth marginal scute distinctly higher than rectangular eighth in adults; triangular pectoral scutes barely in contact; plastron hinged anterior and posterior to abdominal scute.

Similar Species: Eastern mud turtle, common musk turtle.

Subspecies: Variously identified as Illinois mud turtle, *K. f. spooneri*, or yellow mud turtle, *K. f. flavescens*.

Description: Medium-sized (up to 15 cm CL) turtle with dark olive, dark brown, or black carapace and lighter plastron. Vertebral scutes 1–4 mushroom-shaped, broadest anteriorly. Male averages larger than female, with divided patch of rough scales behind knee and longer, heavier tail tipped with a claw. Young with prominent black dot on posterior part of large carapacial scutes and ninth marginal scute higher than eighth.

Habitat: Temporary to permanent ponds and backwaters of rivers in sand prairies and deep sand soils.

Natural History: Burrowed in sand most of year, moving to water a few weeks in spring and early summer. Diet consists of invertebrates, tadpoles, fish, plants. Lays 3–7 ellipsoidal, brittle-shelled eggs (ca. 25 x 15 mm) in burrows between mid-June and July. Predators include hognose snakes, raccoons, foxes, and coyotes.

Status: State endangered. Much original habitat along Green, Illinois, and Mississippi rivers has been destroyed by dredging and lock and dam construction. Current threats include lowered water tables and farming (plowing, draining, irrigating). The Lake County specimens may have been introduced.

Yellow mud turtle (*Kinosternon flavescens*), Cass Co., IL. (MR)

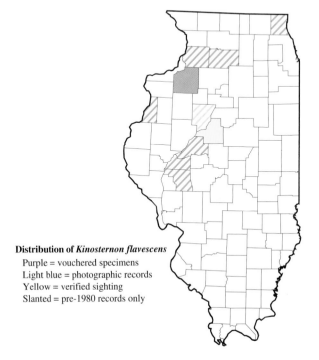

Distribution of *Kinosternon flavescens*
Purple = vouchered specimens
Light blue = photographic records
Yellow = verified sighting
Slanted = pre-1980 records only

Eastern mud turtle
Kinosternon subrubrum

Kinosternidae

Key Characters: Tenth marginal scute highest; eighth and ninth marginal scutes rectangular and of equal height; triangular pectoral scutes barely in contact; plastron hinged anterior and posterior to abdominal scute.

Similar Species: Yellow mud turtle, common musk turtle.

Subspecies: Intergradation between the Eastern mud turtle, *K. s. subrubrum*, and the Mississippi mud turtle, *K. s. hippocrepis*.

Description: Small (12 cm CL) turtle with dull brown carapace, scutes sometimes dark bordered. Sides of head spotted or mottled with yellow. Plastron dark brown or tan. Male has divided patch of rough scales behind knee and a larger swollen tail tipped with a claw. Hatchling tiny (2.0–2.5 cm CL) with a dark carapace and an orange, red, or yellow plastron bearing an extensive patch of dark pigment.

Habitat: Shallow stagnant or slow-moving habitats: wetlands, backwaters, oxbows, cypress swamps. Frequents temporary water, wanders overland.

Natural History: Omnivorous, forages along bottom in shallows for mollusks, crustaceans, insects, and plants. Lays 2–5 ellipsoidal (ca. 30 x 17 mm), brittle-shelled eggs in and under debris or in burrows excavated using the front and hind limbs. Commonly estivates and hibernates in burrows on land.

Status: Uncommon. Drainage of woodland ponds and wetlands in the southern tip of the state constitutes an important threat.

Eastern mud turtle (*Kinosternon subrubrum*), Gallatin Co., IL. (SB)

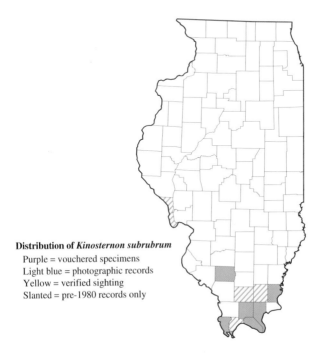

Distribution of *Kinosternon subrubrum*

Purple = vouchered specimens
Light blue = photographic records
Yellow = verified sighting
Slanted = pre-1980 records only

Common musk turtle

Kinosternidae

Sternotherus odoratus

Key Characteristics: Plastron with single, weakly developed hinge anterior to abdominal scute; some plastral scutes separated by soft fleshy tissue in adults; pectoral scutes squarish, contacting broadly at midline.

Similar Species: Yellow mud turtle, common mud turtle.

Description: Small (up to 13 cm CL) turtle with unpatterned, light brown to black carapace. Plastron light brown to yellow. Two light stripes on side of head (fade in old individuals). Barbels on chin and throat. Shell steeply peaked with prominent keel in young, becoming more rounded (with less obvious keel) with age. Male differs from female by having a large, swollen tail tipped with a claw, a divided patch of rough scales behind the knee, and greater amounts of soft tissue between plastral scutes.

Habitat: Permanently aquatic. Mud-bottomed habitats preferred (lakes, ponds, swamps, and slow-moving streams and rivers).

Natural History: Bottom dweller that sometimes emerges onto logs or climbs shoreline bushes to surprising heights to bask. Foods include plants, mollusks, insects, and worms (often from a fisherman's hook). Lays 4 to 5 elliptical (ca. 27 x 15 mm), brittle-shelled eggs up to three times during the May to July nesting season. Named for odiferous substances expelled from glands near the bridge of the shell.

Status: Particularly common in the southern third of Illinois.

Common musk turtle (*Sternotherus odoratus*), Gallatin Co., IL. (EOM)

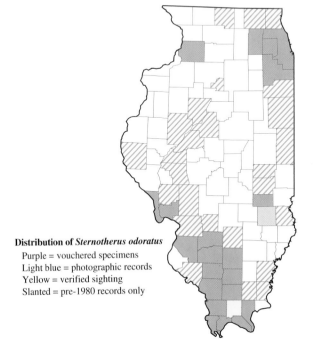

Distribution of *Sternotherus odoratus*

Purple = vouchered specimens
Light blue = photographic records
Yellow = verified sighting
Slanted = pre-1980 records only

Smooth softshell turtle   **Trionychidae**
Apalone mutica

Key Characters: Anterior edge of carapace lacking spines or tubercles; snout with rounded tip; nostrils lacking horizontal septal projections.

Similar Species: Spiny softshell.

Subspecies: Midland smooth softshell, *A. m. mutica*.

Description: Medium-sized (up to 28 cm CL) turtle with tan, brown, or olive carapace with light posterior border. Carapace irregularly patterned with small dark spots or dashes that expand into blotches or mottling in large females. Plastron white to cream. Paired, dark-bordered, white stripes extend across snout to eyes. A similar but expanded pair of stripes extend posteriorly from eyes onto the neck. Feet neither strongly streaked nor patterned. Male smaller than female and has a larger, thicker tail with vent opening beyond rear edge of carapace.

Habitat: Rivers and large streams having sand substrate, bars, and banks. Unusual in lakes.

Natural History: Males and juveniles congregate in sandy shallows to bury in the substrate and bask along exposed banks. Female is more solitary, wanders more, and utilizes deeper water than male. Relatively nonagressive. The diet includes a variety of animal foods but especially aquatic insects. Female lays multiple clutches of 6 to 26 round, brittle-shelled eggs (ca. 22 mm diameter) in sand banks or bars from late May into July.

Status: Unlisted, but populations appear to be declining in much of the state. Agricultural runoff, siltation, and pollution are probable causes.

Smooth softshell turtle (*Apalone mutica*), Gallatin Co., IL. (EOM)

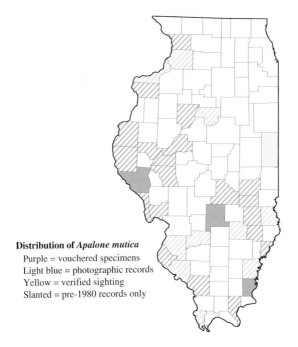

Distribution of *Apalone mutica*

Purple = vouchered specimens
Light blue = photographic records
Yellow = verified sighting
Slanted = pre-1980 records only

Spiny softshell turtle
Apalone spinifera

Trionychidae

Key Characters: Anterior margin of carapace decked with small spines or tubercles; conspicuously patterned feet; snout squared off with horizontal ridge projecting from median septum into each nostril.

Similar Species: Smooth softshell.

Subspecies: Eastern spiny softshell, *A. s. spinifera.*

Description: Large (up to 38 cm CL) turtle with carapace pattern of dark circles and spots in males and juveniles; larger, irregular blotches in females. A pair of dark-bordered light stripes runs from snout to eyes; another pair of similar stripes extends posteriorly from the eye onto the neck; a third pair of short light stripes extends back from mandible. Male smaller with rough sandpaperlike carapace, and conspicuously longer, thicker tail than female.

Habitat: Rivers, backwaters, lakes, and ponds.

Natural History: Often seen basking on logs. Readily bites. Its sharp-edged jaws, hidden beneath the fleshy lips, can deliver a painful wound. Feeds on aquatic insects, crustaceans, and fish. May actively forage for prey or bury itself in the sand to wait for unwary animals to come within striking range. Female nests in sand or mud from mid-May into July, lays an average of 18 round, brittle-shelled eggs (ca. 28 mm) per clutch, up to four clutches per year.

Status: Less susceptible to siltation and pollution than the smooth softshell. Remains common in most river systems within the state.

Spiny softshell turtle (*Apalone spinifera*), Will Co., IL. (MR)
(Inset) Union Co., IL. (MR)

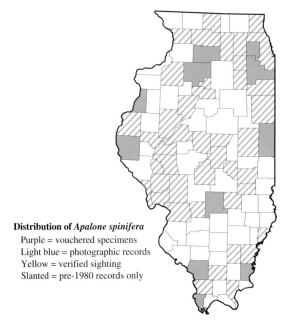

Distribution of *Apalone spinifera*
  Purple = vouchered specimens
  Light blue = photographic records
  Yellow = verified sighting
  Slanted = pre-1980 records only

ORDER SQUAMATA, SUBORDER SAURIA — LIZARDS

Lizards are most often confused with salamanders because of similarities in overall body plan (usually four limbs and a long tail). The exceptional glass lizard (*Ophisaurus attenuatus*) is a limbless burrowing species. In contrast to the smooth-skinned, moist salamanders, however, all lizards are covered with dry scales. All of the lizards in Illinois except one are small to medium-sized and, therefore, are inconspicuous. There are only six native species of lizard in Illinois representing four families: the fence lizard (family Phrynosomatidae), three skinks (family Scincidae), the six-lined racerunner (family Teiidae), and the legless slender glass lizard (family Anguidae). A seventh species, the collared lizard, has been introduced into a small portion of Johnson County. Lizards are most abundant in the southern third of the state in forests, glades, and rocky bluffs.

Distinguishing between two of the three skinks can be difficult and relies on detailed counts of very small head scales; the third is rather distinctive. No lizard is listed as endangered or threatened in Illinois.

In the species accounts, size is given in "cm TL," which is the straight line length in centimeters from the tip of the nose to the end of the tail. Maximum size is the greatest TL recorded in Illinois, unless otherwise stated.

Slender glass lizard   **Anguidae**
Ophisaurus attenuatus

Key Characters: Limbs absent; dark longitudinal stripes flank a noticeable groove on each side of the body.

Similar Species: May be distinguished from snakes by the presence of movable eyelids and external ear openings.

Subspecies: Western slender glass lizard, *O. a. attenuatus.*

Description: A long (up to 90 cm TL), slender lizard with yellow to brown back sporting six longitudinal stripes, including a distinct middorsal stripe. White flecks in the middle of the scales sometimes form light stripes.

Habitat: Prairies, sand prairies, old fields, and dry open woodlands.

Natural History: Known as the glass lizard because of the easily broken tail. Glass lizards eat invertebrates and small lizards. Mating occurs in May and 5 to 15 eggs are laid in late June or July. Hatchlings range from 10 to 13 cm TL. Hawks and carnivorous mammals are the main predators.

Status: The slender glass lizard is not listed as threatened in Illinois although it is seldom encountered.

Slender glass lizard (*Ophisaurus attenuatus*), Will Co., IL. (MR)

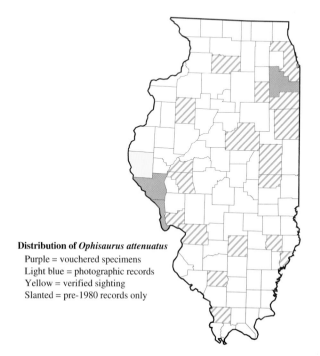

Distribution of *Ophisaurus attenuatus*
Purple = vouchered specimens
Light blue = photographic records
Yellow = verified sighting
Slanted = pre-1980 records only

Fence lizard   **Phrynosomatidae**
Sceloporus undulatus

Key Characters: Rough, spiny scales; dark, wavy, transverse bands on the back.

Similar Species: A distinctive species not easily confused.

Subspecies: Northern fence lizard, *S. u. hyacinthinus*.

Description: A medium-sized (up to 19 cm TL), stout lizard with gray to brown back sporting 5 to 8 dark bands. Belly white with varying amounts of blue or greenish blue along ventral edges. Blue patch on throat. The colored areas on the throat and sides of body are more brilliant in breeding males.

Habitat: Rocky, wooded areas, dry hillsides, and sunny, open woodlots.

Natural History: Mating occurs in April or May. Five to 15 eggs are laid in soil and rotting logs and under surface debris in June, July, or early August. Hatchlings (ca. 4 to 5 cm TL) are usually first seen in late August. The main food items are insects, but other invertebrates are also eaten. Predators include snakes and birds.

Status: Locally abundant, especially in the southern third of the state.

Fence lizard (*Sceloporus undulatus*), Jackson Co., IL. (MR)

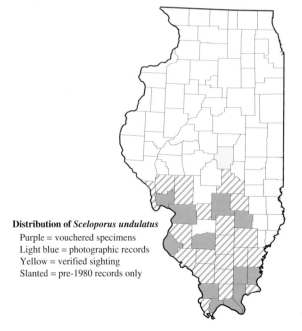

Distribution of *Sceloporus undulatus*
Purple = vouchered specimens
Light blue = photographic records
Yellow = verified sighting
Slanted = pre-1980 records only

Collared lizard   **Crotaphytidae**
Crotaphytus collaris

Key Characters: Large head; narrow neck; long, round tail; two black collars on the back of the neck.

Similar Species: A distinctive species not easily confused.

Subspecies: Eastern collared lizard, *C. c. collaris*.

Description: A large (up to 35 cm TL), green, blue-green, or straw yellow lizard with a light belly and an orange or yellow throat. Back usually covered with small light spots (except in juveniles, which have dark crossbands). Male much brighter than female.

Habitat: Bluffs, rock ledges, and rocky forest openings (glades).

Natural History: This lizard looks like it would be more at home in the deserts of Arizona than in Illinois. Male frequently sits on the top of the highest rock in its home range as if to advertise its presence. Mating takes place in the spring and eggs are laid in late June to July. Clutch size is normally 3–10 eggs and the hatchlings (ca. 9 cm TL) appear in August or September. Collared lizards feed on insects (especially grasshoppers) and small lizards. The main predators are snakes and hawks.

Status: State watch list (status undetermined). This lizard is known from a single locality in Johnson County. It was almost certainly introduced there in the early 1990s.

Collared lizard (*Crotaphytus collaris*), Johnson Co., IL. (MR)

Distribution of *Crotaphytus collaris*
Purple = vouchered specimens
Light blue = photographic records
Yellow = verified sighting
Slanted = pre-1980 records only

Ground skink
Scincidae
Scincella lateralis

Key Characters: Smooth scales; short limbs; a small transparent membrane on the lower eyelid; no supranasal scales.

Similar Species: A distinctive species not easily confused.

Description: A small (up to 13 cm TL), slender copper to chocolate brown lizard with a darker brown dorsolateral stripe on each side. Belly white.

Habitat: Forest and forest edge.

Natural History: Mating takes place in the spring and eggs are laid in late June to July. Clutch size is normally 1–5 eggs and hatching takes place in August or September. Hatchlings average 4 cm TL. Prey includes insects, spiders, and earthworms. The main predators are snakes and small birds.

Status: Common, especially in extreme southern Illinois.

Ground skink (*Scincella lateralis*), Kentucky. (SB)

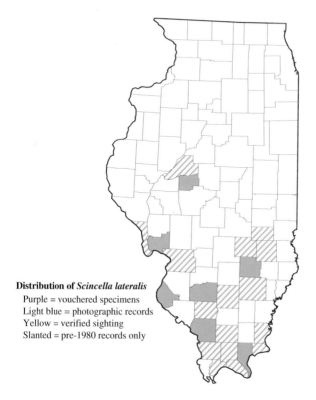

Distribution of *Scincella lateralis*
Purple = vouchered specimens
Light blue = photographic records
Yellow = verified sighting
Slanted = pre-1980 records only

Five-lined skink   **Scincidae**
Eumeces fasciatus

Key Characters: Smooth body scales; seven supralabial scales; two postlabial scales.

Similar Species: Broadhead skink.

Description: A medium-sized (up to 20 cm TL) lizard. Color and pattern depend on age and sex. Juvenile and subadult have a dark back with five longitudinal light lines and a blue tail. Adult female is similar but tail is not blue. Adult male loses stripes with age, eventually becoming uniform olive or brown. Jaws of male become swollen and orange to red during breeding.

Habitat: Wooded habitats including dry uplands, floodplains, and hardwood swamps. Also found on abandoned buildings and around trash piles.

Natural History: Mating occurs in May with eggs laid from late June to July. Two to 18 eggs are laid in sawdust piles, under fallen logs, and under leaf litter. Female usually remains with eggs until hatching. Hatchlings range from 6 to 7 cm TL. Arthropods are the main prey. Predators include birds of prey and small mammals.

Status: Locally common in the southern third of the state.

Five-lined skink (*Eumeces fasciatus*), Union Co., IL. (MR)

Distribution of *Eumeces fasciatus*
  Purple = vouchered specimens
  Light blue = photographic records
  Yellow = verified sighting
  Slanted = pre-1980 records only

Broadhead skink
Eumeces laticeps

Scincidae

Key Characters: Smooth body scales; eight supralabial scales; one postlabial scale.

Similar Species: Five-lined skink.

Description: A large (up to 25 cm TL), stout lizard similar in color and pattern to the five-lined skink.

Habitat: Open forests and around barns and outbuildings near forest edge.

Natural History: One of the most arboreal lizards in Illinois. Adults usually climb high into the nearest tree when disturbed. Mating occurs in May with eggs laid from late June to July. Five to 20 eggs are laid in sawdust piles, under fallen logs, and under leaf litter. Females usually remain with the eggs until hatching. Hatchlings range in size from 6 to 8 cm TL. Arthropods are the main prey. Predators include birds of prey and small mammals.

Status: Locally common in the southern third of the state.

Broadhead skink (*Eumeces laticeps*), Monroe Co., IL. (SB)

Distribution of *Eumeces laticeps*
Purple = vouchered specimens
Light blue = photographic records
Yellow = verified sighting
Slanted = pre-1980 records only

Six-lined racerunner
Teiidae

Cnemidophorus sexlineatus

Key Characters: Small smooth scales on back; eight rows of large rectangular scales on belly; tail usually longer than body.

Similar Species: Five-lined skink.

Subspecies: Six-lined racerunner, *C. s. sexlineatus.*

Description: A long (up to 20 cm TL), slender lizard with olive to brown back with six longitudinal stripes that may be white, light gray, yellow, or blue. Most stripes extend to the base of the tail. Belly is white and in male may be washed with blue. Juvenile is similar to adult but has a light blue tail.

Habitat: Sand prairies, hill prairies, and rocky open habitats.

Natural History: This alert and quick lizard is difficult to capture. Mating takes place in the spring and 3–5 eggs are laid from early June to July. Hatching takes place in early August. Hatchlings average 3 cm TL. Prey include insects and snails. The main predators are snakes.

Status: Rare in the northern hill prairies but common in other parts of its range, especially the Shawnee Hills (Fig. 1).

Six-lined racerunner (*Cnemidophorus sexlineatus*), Will Co., IL. (MR)

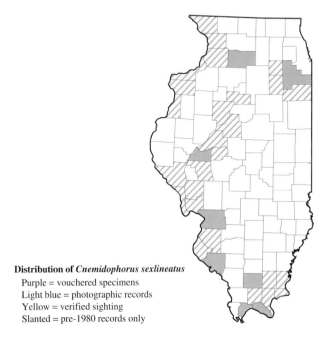

Distribution of *Cnemidophorus sexlineatus*
  Purple = vouchered specimens
  Light blue = photographic records
  Yellow = verified sighting
  Slanted = pre-1980 records only

ORDER SQUAMATA,
SUBORDER SERPENTES —
SNAKES

Snakes can be confused only with legless lizards; however, snakes lack eyelids and ear openings. In Illinois there are 38 snake species representing two families. The majority (34 species) are in one family, the Colubridae, and the remaining 4 species are the venomous vipers (family Viperidae). Snakes can be found in every natural habitat in Illinois, and are often encountered basking in sunny areas or crossing highways as they move to and from den sites in the spring and fall.

Useful characteristics for identifying snakes include whether each scale has a ridge down the middle (keeled) or not (smooth) and whether the scale over the anal opening is single or divided. All snakes in Illinois have small overlapping scales on the back and sides and wide, rectangular plates on the belly. Coloration and pattern on the belly often contrast with the back and sides.

A number of snakes in Illinois are of conservation concern, notably the venomous species. Many are killed out of fear and ignorance, but the majority are killed inadvertently by automobiles on highways. Other snakes that are of conservation concern include species whose ranges barely include Illinois: the western hognose, a relic from an earlier climatic era, and Kirtland's snake, a species restricted to undisturbed wet prairie.

In the species accounts that follow, size is given in "cm TL," which is the straight line length from the tip of the nose to the end of the tail, given in centimeters. The maximum size listed in the "Key Characters" section for each species is the greatest TL recorded for Illinois specimens unless otherwise stated.

Worm snake
Carphophis amoenus

Colubridae

Key Characters: Pointed head; spine-like tail tip; smooth dorsal scales; divided anal plate.

Similar Species: Smooth earth snake, brown snake, redbelly snake.

Subspecies: Midwest worm snake, *C. a. helenae*; western worm snake, *C. a. vermis*.

Description: A small (up to 35 cm TL) wormlike burrowing snake with a brown back and pink belly. The pink color extends onto the first scale row. The two colors are more sharply contrasting in juveniles.

Habitat: Wooded areas, usually those with rocky soils.

Natural History: Most mating probably occurs in the fall with eggs laid the following June. Clutch size is normally 2–5 eggs and hatching takes place in August or September. Hatchlings range in size from 7 to 12 cm TL. Worm snakes feed almost entirely on earthworms. The main predators are other snakes.

Status: Locally abundant.

Worm snake (*Carphophis amoenus*), Alexander Co., IL. (MR)

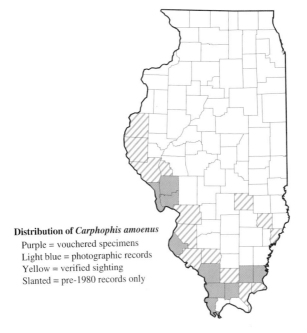

Distribution of *Carphophis amoenus*
Purple = vouchered specimens
Light blue = photographic records
Yellow = verified sighting
Slanted = pre-1980 records only

Scarlet snake   **Colubridae**
Cemophora coccinea

Key Characters: Projecting rounded snout; smooth back scales; anal plate not divided.

Similar Species: Milk snake.

Subspecies: Northern scarlet snake, *C. c. copei.*

Description: Small (up to 60 cm TL), slender, brightly banded snake. Back is white, cream, or yellow with large black-bordered red blotches. Head red, with dark crossbar near eyes, and barely broader than neck. Rostral scale enlarged and projects beyond lower jaw. Belly clear white or cream.

Habitat: Mixed woodlands on rocky, sandy soils.

Natural History: Semifossorial snake that spends most daylight hours buried in sand or under leaf litter, rotten logs, rocks, and other cover. In other states, eggs have been found buried in sand and pine needles late June through August. The 2–9 eggs per clutch probably hatch in September. Hatchlings range from 13 to 18 cm TL. Eats reptile eggs, insects, frogs, lizards, snakes, and mice. Main predators are other snakes, birds, and mammals.

Status: Not listed as endangered because existence in Illinois remains uncertain despite isolated records from Indiana and Missouri. Known in Illinois from one specimen collected in 1942 by Fred R. Cagle at Wolf Lake Swamp, Union County, and originally identified as a red milk snake. The specimen subsequently was correctly identified by Philip W. Smith, noted herpetologist at the Illinois Natural History Survey. Searches in the vicinity of Wolf Lake and nearby Pine Hills have yielded no additional specimens.

Scarlet snake (*Cemophora coccinea*), South Carolina. (RWV)

Distribution of *Cemophora coccinea*

Purple = vouchered specimens
Light blue = photographic records
Yellow = verified sighting
Slanted = pre-1980 records only

Kirtland's snake
Clonophis kirtlandii

Colubridae

Key Characters: Red or orange belly bearing a contrasting row of black spots along each side; keeled scales; divided anal plate.

Similar Species: Brown snake, redbelly snake.

Description: Small (up to 47 cm TL), stout snake with gray or brown back sporting four rows of 46–57 rounded black blotches. Belly bright red to faded orange and distinctively marked by two rows of dark spots. Juvenile darker on the back and sides, and less conspicuously blotched.

Habitat: Prairie wetlands, wet meadows, and grassy edges of creeks, ditches, and ponds, usually in association with crayfish burrows. Has been found in damp habitat remnants in vacant lots of urban settings.

Natural History: Secretive and nocturnal, it shelters beneath logs and surface debris, or in crayfish burrows, by day. When threatened, it flattens its body and becomes rigid. This viviparous snake mates in May and gives birth to 4–15 young in August or September. Newborn are 10–17 cm TL. Diet includes earthworms, leeches, and slugs. Predators include other snakes and birds.

Status: Threatened in Illinois. Known from only a few isolated populations scattered through central and northeastern counties. Threats include drainage of wetlands, destruction of native prairie marshlands, and reduction of earthworm populations by herbicides and pesticides.

Kirtland's snake (*Clonophis kirtlandii*), Sangamon Co., IL. (SB)
(Inset) *C. kirtlandii* belly pattern. (CAP)

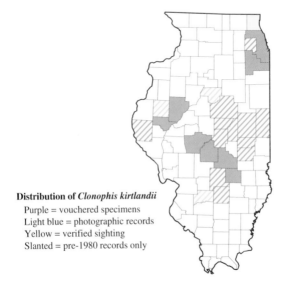

Distribution of *Clonophis kirtlandii*
  Purple = vouchered specimens
  Light blue = photographic records
  Yellow = verified sighting
  Slanted = pre-1980 records only

Racer
Coluber constrictor

Colubridae

Key Characters: Plain black or bluish black; smooth scales; divided anal plate; juveniles heavily marked with small blotches.

Similar Species: Adults resemble the rat snake, coachwhip, and plainbelly water snake; juveniles resemble young of rat, coachwhip, fox, prairie king, milk, and water snakes.

Subspecies: Blue racer, *C. c. foxii*; southern black racer, *C. c. priapus*.

Description: Adult long (up to 150 cm TL) and slender with shiny, uniformly blue, blue-green, or black back. Belly yellowish white to slate gray. Throat distinctly lighter (yellow in northwest, white elsewhere). Hatchling and juvenile up to about 80 cm TL, blue-gray with 55–85 reddish brown blotches on back that become less distinct toward tail, and small dark spots along sides and belly.

Habitat: A variety of habitats including forests, open areas, and edges of forests near open fields.

Natural History: Alert and agile, often raises its head above the ground to look around, and reacts to disturbance by moving away quickly. If cornered, vibrates the tail tip and can be counted on to strike repeatedly. Mates in May and June and female lays 10–20 eggs in late June or July. The young, 20–35 cm TL, hatch in September. Eats a variety of animals, including arthropods, worms, amphibians, reptiles, birds, and small mammals. Main predators are other snakes and raptors.

Status: Locally common in some parts of the state.

Racer (*Coluber constrictor*), Jackson Co., IL. (SB)

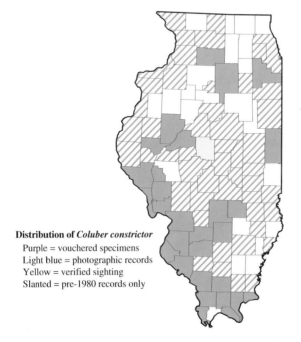

Distribution of *Coluber constrictor*

Purple = vouchered specimens
Light blue = photographic records
Yellow = verified sighting
Slanted = pre-1980 records only

Ringneck snake   **Colubridae**
Diadophis punctatus

Key Characters: Yellow or cream-colored ring around the
neck; dorsal scales smooth; anal plate divided.

Similar Species: No other small snake in Illinois has a ring on
the neck and smooth scales.

Subspecies: Prairie ringneck snake, *D. p. arnyi*; northern
ringneck snake, *D. p. edwardsii*; Mississippi ringneck snake,
D. p. stictogenys.

Description: A small (up to 40 cm TL), wormlike, burrowing
snake with a blue-gray to black back. The belly is yellow or
orange, possibly scattered with black spots or bands. Juvenile
may be darker above than adult. The three subspecies differ in
the extent and location of ventral spots: the prairie ringneck has
numerous irregularly placed spots, the Mississippi ringneck has
paired dark spots down the middle of the belly, and the northern
ringneck's belly has a few black dots or is unmarked.

Habitat: Hill prairies, bluffs, and open forests.

Natural History: Usually found under rocks or debris. Mating
may take place in spring or fall with eggs laid in June. Clutch
size is normally 3–4 eggs and hatching takes place in August or
September. Hatchlings range from 8 to 11 cm TL. Ringnecks
feed on earthworms, small insects, and salamanders. The main
predators are other snakes and birds.

Status: Locally abundant in the Shawnee Hills (Fig. 1) and
along the southern Mississippi River bluffs.

Ringneck snake (*Diadophis punctatus*), Greene Co., IL. (MR)

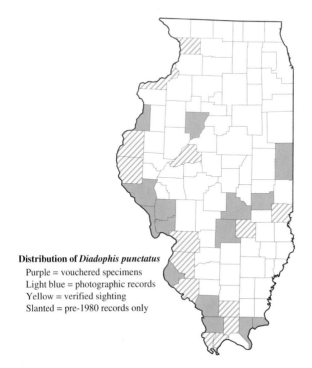

Distribution of *Diadophis punctatus*
Purple = vouchered specimens
Light blue = photographic records
Yellow = verified sighting
Slanted = pre-1980 records only

Corn snake
Elaphe guttata

Colubridae

Key Characters: Spear-shaped pattern on top of head; body scales keeled; anal plate divided.

Similar Species: Prairie kingsnake, milk snake, fox snake, rat snake.

Subspecies: Great Plains rat snake, *E. g. emoryi.*

Description: Moderately large (up to 120 cm TL), blotched snake with gray or light brown back sporting 25 to 50 black-bordered, nearly square, dark brown or red-brown blotches. Tail with 8–20 dark spots or bands. Belly checkered black and white.

Habitat: Rocky, wooded hillsides, hill prairies, bluffs, and adjacent brushy fields.

Natural History: This nocturnal snake mates in April or May and lays 3–30 eggs a few weeks later. The young, 30–35 cm TL, hatch in August. Diet includes mammals, birds, and bird eggs. Medium-sized mammals and raptors are the main predators.

Status: Threatened in Illinois. Found only along the Mississippi River bluffs from Jersey to Randolph counties, where its main threat is highway traffic.

Corn snake (*Elaphe guttata*), Monroe Co., IL. (MR)

Distribution of *Elaphe guttata*

Purple = vouchered specimens
Light blue = photographic records
Yellow = verified sighting
Slanted = pre-1980 records only

Rat snake
Elaphe obsoleta

Colubridae

Key Characters: Sides unusually straight, forming a sharp corner with the belly; back scales weakly keeled; anal plate divided. Juvenile distinctly marked with dark back and side blotches on a white or gray background.

Similar Species: Racer, common kingsnake, plainbelly water snake. Juvenile resembles many blotched snakes: milk snake, young of prairie kingsnake, racer, coachwhip, and water snakes.

Subspecies: Black rat snake, *E. o. obsoleta*; gray rat snake, *E. o. spiloides*.

Description: Large (up to 175 cm TL), dark snake with a highly variable pattern that ranges from a series of light blotches to completely black. The groundcolor between blotches darkens with age, obscuring most of them by 80 cm TL, except in extreme southern counties where the subspecies *E. o. spiloides* retains remnants of the juvenile pattern throughout life. Belly black-and-white-checkered. Adults have white, orange, or red skin between the dark scales.

Habitat: Variety of forest, shrub, and edge habitats. Common around farm buildings and abandoned houses.

Natural History: This arboreal constrictor often suns and prowls on tree limbs and rock outcrops where it feeds on birds, their eggs, and small mammals. Mates in April or June and lays 10–20 eggs between early May and July. Young (ca. 30–35 cm TL) hatch late July to September. Large adults have few predators other than humans. Carnivorous mammals and raptors are the main predators of juveniles.

Status: Locally common, especially in southern counties.

Rat snake (*Elaphe obsoleta*), Alexander Co., IL. (MR)

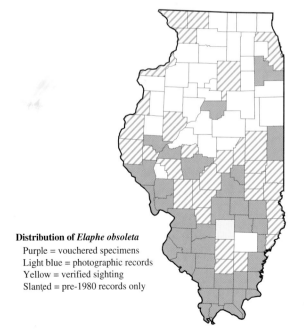

Distribution of *Elaphe obsoleta*

Purple = vouchered specimens
Light blue = photographic records
Yellow = verified sighting
Slanted = pre-1980 records only

Fox snake
Elaphe vulpina

Colubridae

Key Characters: Back yellow with brown blotches; belly black with yellow checks; back scales weakly keeled; anal plate divided.

Similar Species: Prairie kingsnake, milk snake, rat snake, Great Plains rat snake, bullsnake.

Subspecies: Western fox snake, *E. v. vulpina.*

Description: Large (up to 130 cm TL) snake with copper-colored head distinctly wider than neck. Back yellow to bronze with 34–42 reddish brown blotches and an alternating row of brown spots along each side. Belly yellow and boldly marked with black. Hatchling and juvenile resemble adult except for having gray ground coloring and black or dark chestnut blotches.

Habitat: Variety of open and former prairie habitats, including intensively cultivated fields and pastures, in the northern half of the state.

Natural History: A diurnal constrictor that, like many other snakes, often vibrates its tail when threatened. Active early spring through late autumn, even on warm winter days when drawn from its underground hibernation. Mates from June to early July and lays 8–27 eggs about 30 days later. Young (ca. 23–30 cm TL) hatch in late August or September. Diet includes small mammals, birds, their eggs, and nestlings. Main predators are carnivorous mammals and raptors.

Status: Locally common, especially in Grand Prairie (Fig. 1).

Fox snake (*Elaphe vulpina*), Will Co., IL. (MR)

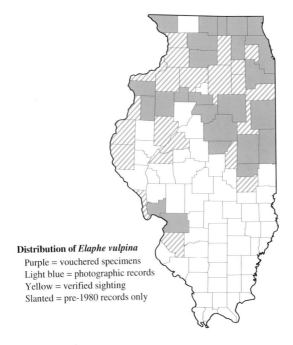

Distribution of *Elaphe vulpina*

Purple = vouchered specimens
Light blue = photographic records
Yellow = verified sighting
Slanted = pre-1980 records only

Mud snake   **Colubridae**
Farancia abacura

Key Characters: Red and black bars on belly; hard, spurlike tail tip; back scales smooth and shiny; anal plate divided.

Similar Species: Copperbelly water snake.

Subspecies: Western mud snake, *F. a. reinwardtii.*

Description: Large (up to 150 cm TL) glossy black snake with alternating red and black bars on lower sides and belly, and small eyes. Male has a more bulbous tail and an area of smaller, keeled scales on the back above the vent.

Habitat: Shallow ponds, sloughs, and swamps containing rotting logs in the Coastal Plain (Fig. 1) of extreme southern counties. Often crosses roads on rainy nights.

Natural History: Mating takes place in midsummer and eggs are laid a few weeks later. Clutches of 4–104 eggs hatch in August or September. Hatchlings 18–24 cm TL resemble adults in coloration. Diet of this nocturnal snake consists entirely of amphibians: salamanders and their larvae, tadpoles, and frogs. Large wading birds and medium-sized mammals are the main predators, especially of the young. This snake has the startling defensive behavior of pushing its hard tail tip against the hand of someone holding it. This apparently is the "hoop snake" of folklore.

Status: Not listed as endangered or threatened in Illinois, but it is seldom seen even where populations are thought to be secure.

Mud snake (*Farancia abacura*), Union Co., IL. (MR)

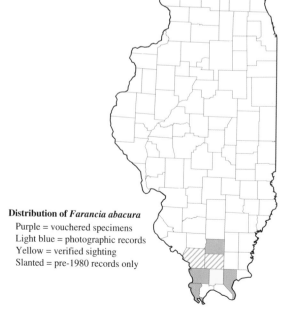

Distribution of *Farancia abacura*
 Purple = vouchered specimens
 Light blue = photographic records
 Yellow = verified sighting
 Slanted = pre-1980 records only

Western hognose snake

Colubridae

Heterodon nasicus

Key Characters: Upturned scale at tip of the nose; belly and underside of tail mainly black; prefrontal scales separated by small scales; back scales keeled; anal plate divided.

Similar Species: Eastern hognose snake.

Subspecies: Dusty hognose snake, *H. n. gloydi*; plains hognose snake, *H. n. nasicus*.

Description: Medium-sized (up to 60 cm TL), stout snake with gray or tan back covered with 35–40 dark blotches. Belly mostly black. Numerous small, unpaired scales on top of the snout (in front of the eyes).

Habitat: Sand prairies, savannas, and adjacent woodlots in well-drained soil.

Natural History: Most often observed crossing sandy roads in brushy or weedy sand prairie remnants. Widens the neck, hisses, and sometimes strikes when disturbed, then rolls onto its back and feigns death. Mates in spring and lays eggs in July. The 8–10 young per clutch hatch in August or September at TL of 17–20 cm. Moves slowly as it searches during the day for toads, other amphibians, reptiles and their eggs, birds, and small mammals, some of which it digs out of sand with its snout. Saliva is toxic to prey, and is injected with enlarged posterior teeth. Main predators are raptors and medium-sized mammals.

Status: Threatened in Illinois. Its main threat is degradation and destruction of sand prairies. There is evidence that the Kankakee County population was introduced.

Western hognose snake
(*Heterodon nasicus*),
Kankakee Co., IL. (CAP)

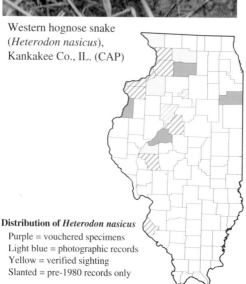

Distribution of *Heterodon nasicus*
Purple = vouchered specimens
Light blue = photographic records
Yellow = verified sighting
Slanted = pre-1980 records only

Eastern hognose snake **Colubridae**
Heterodon platirhinos

Key Characters: Enlarged upturned plate at tip of nose; underside of tail light; back scales keeled; anal plate divided; prefrontal scales contact each other.

Similar Species: Western hognose snake.

Description: Medium-sized (up to 90 cm TL), stout-bodied snake highly variable in coloration and pattern. Usually gray, tan, or brown back with 20–30 dark blotches. Some individuals are olive, brown, or black with no blotches. Belly light or dark, but underside of tail always lighter than belly. Tail short, less than 22% of body length.

Habitat: Forest-edge habitats and dry, open woods on clay or sandy loam; sand areas of northern counties.

Natural History: This is the "puff adder" or "hissing viper" of folklore. Defensive behavior resembles that of western hognose snake. When first encountered, it commonly flattens the head and neck, hisses, feigns strikes (striking to the side rather than biting), releases feces and foul-smelling musk, then rolls onto its back with mouth open and appears to have died. If righted, it rolls over again. Mates in spring and lays 8–20 eggs in June, July, or August, the number depending on size of the female. Hatchlings range from 17 to 25 cm TL. Food consists mainly of frogs and toads. Main predators are raptors and other snakes.

Status: Common in regions of major sand deposits. Rare in Grand Prairie (Fig. 1).

Eastern hognose snake (*Heterodon platirhinos*), Jackson Co., IL. (MR)

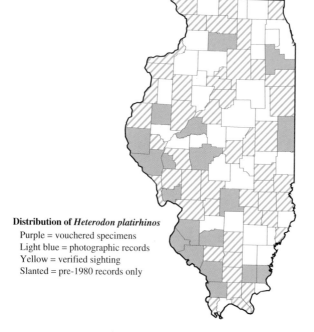

Distribution of *Heterodon platirhinos*
Purple = vouchered specimens
Light blue = photographic records
Yellow = verified sighting
Slanted = pre-1980 records only

Prairie kingsnake   **Colubridae**
Lampropeltis calligaster

Key Characters: Brownish back and sides marked with dark blotches; head not much wider than neck; back scales glossy smooth; anal plate not divided.

Similar Species: Milk snake, rat snake, Great Plains rat snake, fox snake.

Subspecies: Prairie kingsnake, *L. c. calligaster*.

Description: Long (up to 130 cm TL), slender snake with gray to brown back, and 40–64 brown or reddish brown blotches that have dark borders. Two alternating rows of dark spots on sides (some blotches may fuse). Some individuals uniform olive brown, a few striped. Belly cream or yellowish gray with dim dark markings. Young are more distinctly blotched and their bellies more clearly marked with black.

Habitat: Grasslands from high-quality remnant prairie to degraded brushy fields. Less common in heavily farmed black-soil prairie.

Natural History: May become active on warm days even in November and December. Active by day during spring and autumn, but becomes nocturnal during hot summer months. Mates soon after emerging from hibernation in April or May. Clutches of 7–20 eggs laid in midsummer hatch in August and September. Hatchlings are 25–30 cm TL. Diet includes small mammals, birds, amphibians, reptiles, and insects. Main predators are mammals and other snakes.

Status: Locally common in prairie remnants of the Southern Till Plain counties (Fig. 1).

Prairie kingsnake (*Lampropeltis calligaster*), Jackson Co., IL. (MR)

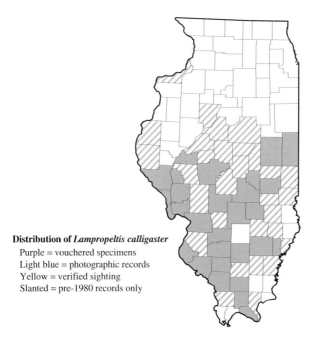

Distribution of *Lampropeltis calligaster*

Purple = vouchered specimens
Light blue = photographic records
Yellow = verified sighting
Slanted = pre-1980 records only

Common kingsnake

Colubridae

Lampropeltis getula

Key Characters: Some or all back and side scales black with a small light dot in the center; belly checkered black and yellow; back scales smooth; anal plate not divided.

Similar Species: Racer, rat snake, plainbelly water snake.

Subspecies: Speckled kingsnake, *L. g. holbrookii*; black kingsnake, *L. g. niger*.

Description: Large (up to 125 cm TL) glossy black snake with white dot in the center of each scale. In *L. g. niger*, the small light dots form 40–50 narrow crossbands with intervening scales lacking dots.

Habitat: Wooded hills.

Natural History: Mates in spring and lays 8–12 eggs in June in rotting logs or tree stumps. Young hatch in August or early September at 20–30 cm TL. Like many snakes, it is largely nocturnal during summer and more active during the day in spring and autumn. Slow and deliberate in its movements, this is a constricting predator of other reptiles, especially snakes (even venomous ones), lizards and their eggs, birds, and small mammals. Main predators of juveniles are other snakes; main predators of adults are hawks, raccoons, skunks, and opossums.

Status: Locally common in the Shawnee Hills (Fig. 1) and along the southern Mississippi River bluffs.

Common kingsnake (*Lampropeltis getula*), Johnson Co., IL. (MR)

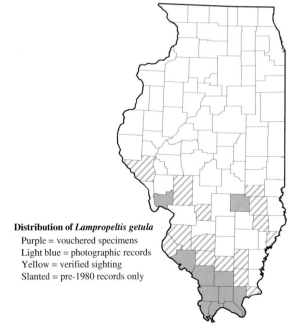

Distribution of *Lampropeltis getula*

Purple = vouchered specimens
Light blue = photographic records
Yellow = verified sighting
Slanted = pre-1980 records only

Milk snake   **Colubridae**
Lampropeltis triangulum

Key Characters: Black-bordered red or brown blotches or
rings; belly white with sharply contrasting black spots; back
scales smooth; anal plate not divided.

Similar Species: Prairie kingsnake, Great Plains rat snake.

Subspecies: Eastern milk snake, *L. t. triangulum*; red milk
snake, *L. t. syspila*.

Description: Medium-sized (up to 110 cm TL) snake with
variable color pattern. The less brightly colored *L. t. triangulum*
has 33–46 brown blotches on the back alternating with 1–2 rows
of spots on the side. The brighter *L. t. syspila* has 19–26 red
blotches on the back and 4–8 red rings on the tail.

Habitat: A variety of habitats from rocky, wooded hillsides and
glades to old fields and wetlands.

Natural History: Usually found in rotting logs, under bark of
stumps, or under logs, rocks, and other surface debris. Mates in
spring and lays 8–20 eggs in June in rotting logs, tree stumps, or
other rotting vegetation. The young hatch in August or early
September at 20-25 cm TL. Diet includes small mammals, birds
and bird eggs, reptiles and reptile eggs, frogs, and fish. Predators
include birds of prey and mammals, but many more probably are
killed on roads by vehicles.

Status: Not commonly seen, except perhaps in the Chicago
region and portions of the Shawnee Hills (Fig. 1), because of its
secretive nature. Red milk snakes may be over-collected for the
pet trade at some localities.

Red milk snake (*Lampropeltis triangulum syspila*), Monroe Co., IL. (MR)
(Inset) Eastern milk snake (*Lampropeltis t. triangulum*), Cook Co., IL. (MR)

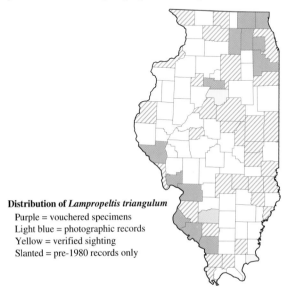

Distribution of *Lampropeltis triangulum*
Purple = vouchered specimens
Light blue = photographic records
Yellow = verified sighting
Slanted = pre-1980 records only

Coachwhip   **Colubridae**
Masticophis flagellum

Key Characters: Tail scales patterned like a braided whip; back scales smooth; anal plate divided.

Similar Species: Racer, rat snake.

Subspecies: Eastern coachwhip, *M. f. flagellum.*

Description: Long (up to 260 cm TL), slender, black snake. Adult uniformly black above and below, fading toward the reddish or tan tail. Juvenile yellow to brown on the back, with dark crossbands; belly cream with rows of brown spots and head marked with white.

Habitat: Rocky, open hillsides, glades, and hill prairies.

Natural History: Fast-moving diurnal snake that is difficult to capture, but tales of it wrapping around people's legs and whipping them with its tail are fictitious. If it cannot escape, it strikes and bites, often aiming for the face, and sprays feces and musk. Withstands dry habitats because it is quite resistant to desiccation. Mates in spring soon after emergence from hibernation and lays 4–24 eggs in summer. Young (ca. 30–35 cm TL) hatch in September. Varied diet includes insects, lizards, other snakes, birds, small turtles, and small mammals. It tracks prey by scent, following them into burrows or trees. Raptors, mammals, and other snakes are its main predators.

Status: State endangered. Only one population known in southwestern Illinois. Its main threat is highway traffic.

Coachwhip (*Masticophis flagellum*), Missouri. (TRJ)

Distribution of *Masticophis flagellum*
Purple = vouchered specimens
Light blue = photographic records
Yellow = verified sighting
Slanted = pre-1980 records only

Mississippi green water snake   Colubridae
Nerodia cyclopion

Key Characters: Subocular scale between eye and supralabial scales; dark belly covered with pale half-moons; back scales strongly keeled; anal plate divided.

Similar Species: Diamondback water snake, cottonmouth.

Description: Large (up to 100 cm TL), stout snake with greenish black or olive brown back and sides. Fifty barely visible, narrow black crossbands above vague alternating dark blotches. Belly dark brown or black with off-white half-moons. No other water snake in Illinois has the subocular scale.

Habitat: Quiet backwater sloughs and cypress-tupelo swamps of extreme southwestern counties.

Natural History: This viviparous snake mates in May and gives birth to 10–20 young in late July or August. Newborn are 25–27 cm TL. Diet mainly of fish, but also includes amphibians. Predators include other snakes and large shore birds. Water snakes are often killed by people who mistake them for cottonmouths.

Status: Threatened in Illinois. Threats include drainage of sloughs and swamps and removal of aquatic vegetation.

Mississippi green water snake (*Nerodia cyclopion*), Union Co., IL. (MR)

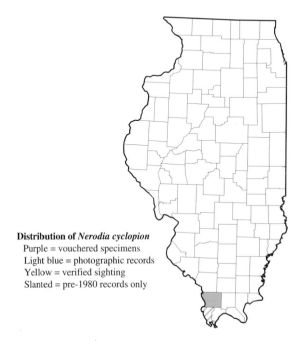

Distribution of *Nerodia cyclopion*
Purple = vouchered specimens
Light blue = photographic records
Yellow = verified sighting
Slanted = pre-1980 records only

Plainbelly water snake   **Colubridae**
Nerodia erythrogaster

Key Characteristics: Yellow or orange unpatterned belly; back scales strongly keeled; anal plate divided; back of newborn marked with black blotches, but darken within a year.

Similar Species: Racer, rat snake, cottonmouth. Juvenile resembles blotched young of many other snakes.

Subspecies: Yellowbelly water snake, *N. e. flavigaster*; copperbelly water snake, *N. e. neglecta*.

Description: Large (up to 140 cm TL), stout snake. Adult is uniformly dark brown or black, juvenile has 30–35 dark blotches. Belly usually yellow with no dark markings in *N. e. flavigaster*, usually bright orange with encroachment of dark side pigment onto belly scales in *N. e. neglecta* (more encroachment in larger individuals).

Habitat: Backwater sloughs, cypress-tupelo swamps, and lowland lakes and ponds with abundant vegetation and muddy bottoms. Often seen in nearby forest.

Natural History: Often leaves water to forage for amphibians. Mates in May and June and gives birth to 10–20 young in late July or August. Newborn are 20–28 cm TL. Diet includes fish and amphibians. Predators include other snakes, large shore birds, mink, and raccoons. Often killed by people who mistake it for cottonmouth.

Status: Through a conservation agreement with the U.S. Fish and Wildlife Service, the copperbelly subspecies is protected as though it were listed in Illinois. Threats include drainage of wetlands, removal of aquatic vegetation, and loss of border habitat suitable for amphibians.

Plainbelly water snake (*Nerodia erythrogaster*), Pope Co., IL. (MR)

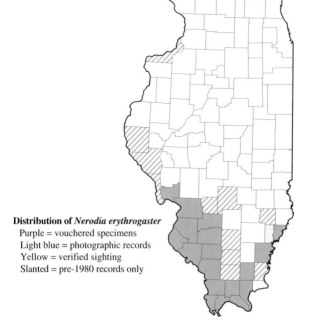

Distribution of *Nerodia erythrogaster*
  Purple = vouchered specimens
  Light blue = photographic records
  Yellow = verified sighting
  Slanted = pre-1980 records only

Southern water snake   **Colubridae**
Nerodia fasciata

Key Characters: Broad black bands or blotches on back; dark line from eye to corner of mouth; back scales strongly keeled; anal plate divided.

Similar Species: Northern water snake.

Subspecies: Broad-banded water snake, *N. f. confluens*.

Description: Large (up to 100 cm TL), stout snake. Back yellowish with 14–26 wide, black or dark brown blotches separated by narrow yellowish orange spaces. Sides marked with 20–35 black or brown blotches. Belly yellow, checkered with black or brown rectangular spots.

Habitat: Quiet backwaters and cypress swamps in extreme southwestern Illinois.

Natural History: A viviparous snake, it mates in April or May and gives birth to 15–20 young in late July or August. Newborn are 14–25 cm TL. Diet consists of fish and amphibians. Predators include other snakes and large shore birds.

Status: Endangered in Illinois. Threats include drainage of wetlands and removal of aquatic vegetation. May be extirpated from the only locality known in the state.

Southern water snake (*Nerodia fasciata*), Tennessee. (MR)

Distribution of *Nerodia fasciata*
Purple = vouchered specimens
Light blue = photographic records
Yellow = verified sighting
Slanted = pre-1980 records only

Diamondback water snake   Colubridae
Nerodia rhombifer

Key Characters: Dark chainlike pattern on the back; back scales strongly keeled; anal plate divided.

Similar Species: Mississippi green water snake, cottonmouth.

Subspecies: Diamondback water snake, *N. r. rhombifer.*

Description: Large (up to 135 cm TL), stout yellow or light green snake with 25–37 dark Y-shaped side markings that meet on the back to enclose a series of light diamonds down the middle of the back. Pattern brightest in juveniles, obscured in some large adults. Belly yellow with dark spots or half-moons that are most numerous toward the tail. Male has conspicuous papillae under the chin.

Habitat: Quiet, permanent backwaters, swamps, sloughs, lakes, and sluggish streams in the southern third of the state, often in very warm water.

Natural History: One of the largest and most pugnacious snakes in Illinois, it bites and defecates repeatedly when handled. Often basks on limbs overhanging water. Active February through September, it hibernates in beaver lodges, muskrat burrows, and mud bottoms. Mates in late April or May and gives birth to 20 or more young from late August through mid-October. Newborn 25–27 cm TL. Diet consists mainly of fish, but frogs are eaten as well. Predators include other snakes and large shore birds. Large numbers are killed by people who mistake them for cottonmouths.

Status: Common along river bottoms and lowland lakes.

Diamondback water snake (*Nerodia rhombifer*), Jackson Co., IL. (MR)

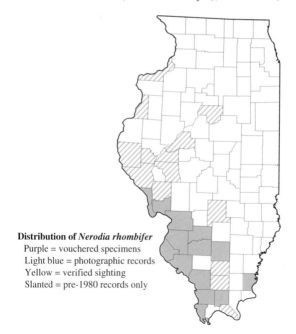

Distribution of *Nerodia rhombifer*
Purple = vouchered specimens
Light blue = photographic records
Yellow = verified sighting
Slanted = pre-1980 records only

Northern water snake   **Colubridae**
Nerodia sipedon

Key Characters: Dark body bands anteriorly, blotches posteriorly; back scales strongly keeled; anal plate divided.

Similar Species: Broad-banded water snake, juvenile plainbelly water snake, cottonmouth, copperhead.

Subspecies: Midland water snake, *N. s. pleuralis*; northern water snake, *N. s. sipedon*.

Description: Large (up to 120 cm TL), stout snake with highly variable dorsal coloration. Back light brown, gray, or tan with about 30 reddish brown or dark brown crossbands and blotches (northern subspecies has more than 30, midland subspecies fewer than 30). Crossbands wider on back than on side, and usually wider than intervening paler areas. Belly light yellow with many red or brown half-moons.

Habitat: Streams, lakes, ponds, and ditches. Commonly seen basking on rocks and logs or foraging in the water. Takes shelter under rocks, logs, and other debris along shore.

Natural History: Like most other water snakes, it readily bites and voids feces when handled. Mates in May and gives birth to 20–50 young in late July or August. Newborn are 15–25 cm TL. Diet consists mainly of fish and amphibians. Predators include other snakes and large shore birds. Many are killed by people who mistake them for cottonmouths (even hundreds of miles north of the range of cottonmouths) or copperheads.

Status: Abundant throughout Illinois in both natural and man-made bodies of water.

Northern water snake (*Nerodia sipedon*), Jackson Co., IL. (MR)

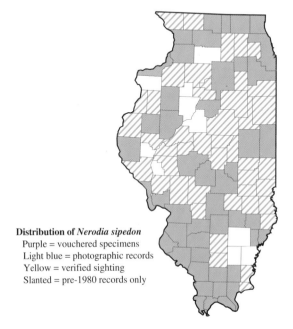

Distribution of *Nerodia sipedon*
  Purple = vouchered specimens
  Light blue = photographic records
  Yellow = verified sighting
  Slanted = pre-1980 records only

Rough green snake   **Colubridae**
Opheodrys aestivus

Key Characters: Seventeen rows of keeled scales at midbody; divided anal plate.

Similar Species: Smooth green snake.

Description: Slender bright green snake up to 85 cm TL with a white or yellowish white belly. Underside of head is light yellow. Head is large compared with slender neck. Long slender tail is over one-third of TL.

Habitat: Inhabitants of small trees, bushes, and vines, especially near lakes and streams along forest edges.

Natural History: Active by day and sleeps at night perched in bushes and shrubs. Well camouflaged against predators on green branches, and transpiring leaves may reduce rate of cutaneous water loss. Moves quickly when disturbed and may open its dark-lined mouth threateningly, but rarely bites. Mates in spring and lays 4–6 elongated, thin-shelled eggs in June and July in rotting logs and stumps, and under flat rocks and other cover. Young 18–21 cm TL hatch in late August or September. Stalks crickets, caterpillars, grasshoppers, spiders, and other soft arthropods by moving slowly along leaves and branches. Main predators are other snakes, birds, and mammals.

Status: Locally abundant in the southern half of the state. May be reduced in some areas where insecticides are applied.

Rough green snake (*Opheodrys aestivus*), Jackson Co., IL. (SB)

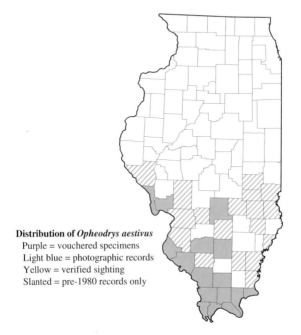

Distribution of *Opheodrys aestivus*
Purple = vouchered specimens
Light blue = photographic records
Yellow = verified sighting
Slanted = pre-1980 records only

Smooth green snake   **Colubridae**
Opheodrys vernalis

Key Characters: Fifteen rows of smooth scales at midbody; divided anal plate.

Similar Species: Rough green snake.

Description: Slender green snake up to 85 cm TL with off-white belly. Newborn is dark olive-green; slightly older juvenile is gray-green.

Habitat: Moist prairie remnants, savannas, bogs, marshes, wet meadows, old fields, and vacant lots.

Natural History: Less arboreal than rough green snake, only occasionally climbing onto low bush branches. Active during the day April to October when it can be found in grass, in low bushes, and under rocks, boards, and other debris. Does not bite when handled, but sometimes feigns striking and voids feces and musk. Hibernates in ant hills, rodent burrows, and other retreats below ground. Mates in May and lays 5–15 thin-shelled eggs in June. Young 8–15 cm TL hatch in August. In northern populations, female incubates eggs internally for a time by basking, then lays them in a mound of rotting plants or in a sawdust pile, rotting log, or rodent burrow. Food consists of spiders, centipedes, millipedes, slugs, snails, and insects. Main predators are other snakes, birds, and mammals.

Status: Not abundant anywhere in the state. Reduced by habitat destruction and widespread use of insecticides that eliminate populations of food organisms.

Smooth green snake (*Opheodrys vernalis*), Cook Co., IL. (MR)

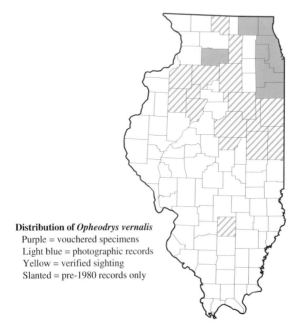

Distribution of *Opheodrys vernalis*
Purple = vouchered specimens
Light blue = photographic records
Yellow = verified sighting
Slanted = pre-1980 records only

Bullsnake
Pituophis melanoleucus

Colubridae

Key Characters: Narrowed snout with an enlarged rostral scale; four prefrontal scales; back scales weakly keeled; anal plate not divided.

Similar Species: Fox snake.

Subspecies: Bullsnake, *P. m. sayi*.

Description: Large (up to 180 cm TL), stout snake with a disproportionately small head. Back yellow to tan with 36–54 black (anterior and posterior) and brown (midbody) blotches that alternate with two rows of dark spots on each side. Tail marked with 8–15 black rings that contrast sharply with yellow-and-black-checkered belly. Juvenile resembles adult except that its back is tanner and back blotches are usually all black.

Habitat: Sand prairies, grasslands, and old fields in former prairie. Absent from the black-muck prairies.

Natural History: Climbs and burrows readily. Well known for its defensive display, which includes tail vibrating, loud hissing, and repeated lunging with the mouth partially open. Mates in April or May and lays about 10 eggs in June, usually in burrows excavated by the female. Communal nesting is common, so large clutches may be from more than one female. Young hatch in August or September at 20–25 cm TL. Its appetite for small rodents makes this snake a friend of farmers. Birds of prey are the likely predators, but many adults are killed by unenlightened people and on roads by vehicles.

Status: Locally common in the extensive sand prairies of central and northwestern counties.

Bullsnake (*Pituophis melanoleucus*), Whiteside Co., IL. (RAB)

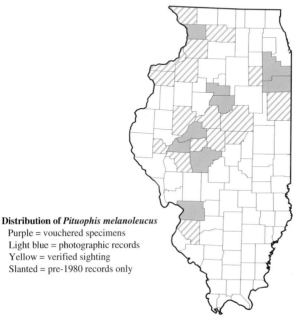

Distribution of *Pituophis melanoleucus*
  Purple = vouchered specimens
  Light blue = photographic records
  Yellow = verified sighting
  Slanted = pre-1980 records only

Graham's crayfish snake   **Colubridae**
Regina grahamii

Key Characters: Yellow stripe on scale rows 1–3; back scales strongly keeled; anal plate divided.

Similar Species: Queen snake.

Description: Medium-sized (up to 100 cm TL), relatively stout-bodied brown or dark olive water snake. Side stripe bordered below by a narrow, irregular black stripe along the outer edges of belly scales. Sometimes a midback light stripe is present. Belly plain yellow or off-white, the hind third with a faint dark line or row of dots down the center. Stripes and belly more yellow and midback light stripe more frequent in juveniles.

Habitat: The still-water, prairie equivalent of the queen snake, it lives in and along banks of soft-bottomed, heavily vegetated lakes, ponds, sluggish streams, sloughs, and roadside ditches.

Natural History: Secretive and difficult to catch, it basks on rock piles and overhanging branches. Hibernates in crayfish burrows and burrows it excavates. Mates in late April or May and gives birth to 10–20 young in late July, August, or September. Newborn 15–25 cm TL. Frequent prey are recently molted crayfish, but fish and frogs also are eaten. Predators include other snakes, large shore birds, and mammals.

Status: Widespread but uncommon. Absent from the Wabash and Ohio river counties.

Graham's crayfish snake (*Regina grahamii*), Clinton Co., IL. (MR)

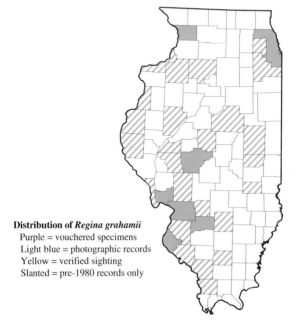

Distribution of *Regina grahamii*
Purple = vouchered specimens
Light blue = photographic records
Yellow = verified sighting
Slanted = pre-1980 records only

Queen snake

Colubridae

Regina septemvittata

Key Characters: Yellow stripe on scale rows 1–2; four dark brown stripes on the belly; back scales strongly keeled; anal plate divided.

Similar Species: Graham's crayfish snake.

Description: Medium-sized (up to 90 cm TL), relatively stout-bodied brown or dark olive water snake. Belly yellow or off-white and boldly marked with two brown stripes down the center and another on each side of belly scales (dark stripes obscured in many older adults).

Habitat: In and along banks of relatively unpolluted, rocky woodland streams where crayfish are abundant.

Natural History: This mainly diurnal snake commonly basks in branches overhanging water, then retreats under rocks in the water, under cover on shore, and down burrows in banks and dams. It mates in late April or May and gives birth to 8–12 young from late July to September. Newborn are 18–20 cm TL. Diet consists almost entirely of soft, recently molted crayfish. Predators include other snakes, shore birds, and mammals. When captured, it seldom bites, but squirms violently and sprays feces and foul-smelling musk.

Status: Uncommon in most of its range, but may be abundant locally in good habitat. Threats include water pollution that reduces crayfish populations and siltation of rocky stream bottoms.

Queen snake (*Regina septemvittata*), Will Co., IL. (MR)

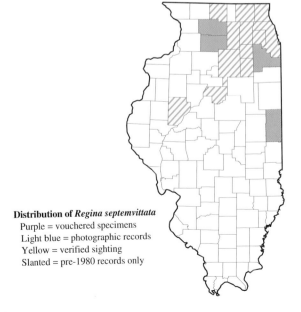

Distribution of *Regina septemvittata*
  Purple = vouchered specimens
  Light blue = photographic records
  Yellow = verified sighting
  Slanted = pre-1980 records only

Brown snake   **Colubridae**
Storeria dekayi

Key Characters: Prominent dark blotch on either side of neck; a dark spot under each eye; one preocular scale; back scales strongly keeled and in 17 rows; anal plate divided.

Similar Species: Redbelly snake, ringneck snake.

Subspecies: Midland brown snake, *S. d. wrightorum.*

Description: Small (up to 45 cm TL) gray or light brown snake with two rows of small, dark spots on the back. On some individuals back spots are connected by side bars to form a ladderlike pattern. Usually a faint light stripe on midback. Belly light pink. Juveniles have a gray or white collar behind the head.

Habitat: Variety of forest and prairie habitats, floodplains and uplands, forest edges, even cultivated fields, and especially in vacant lots in cities.

Natural History: Abundant where there is much surface cover and an abundant supply of food. Mates in April and May and gives birth to 5–25 young from late July through early September. Newborn 5–12 cm TL. Eats mainly earthworms and slugs, and is preyed upon by snakes, birds, mammals, and even large toads and spiders. Large numbers are killed on roads separating cultivated fields from forested rocky bluffs each spring and autumn as they move to and from hibernacula.

Status: Common throughout most of the state.

Brown snake (*Storeria dekayi*), Washington Co., IL. (MR)

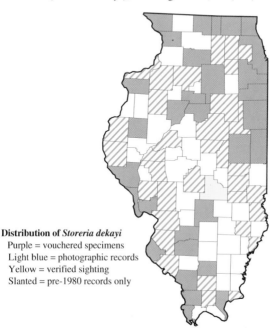

Distribution of *Storeria dekayi*
 Purple = vouchered specimens
 Light blue = photographic records
 Yellow = verified sighting
 Slanted = pre-1980 records only

Redbelly snake   Colubridae
Storeria occipitomaculata

Key Characters: Three light spots just behind the head; plain red belly; two preocular scales; back scales strongly keeled and in 15 rows; anal plate divided.

Similar Species: Brown snake, smooth earth snake, Kirtland's snake.

Subspecies: Northern redbelly snake, *S. o. occipitomaculata.*

Description: Small (up to 35 cm TL), slender black, gray, or light brown snake. Sometimes a faint midback stripe and usually a light blotch on the fifth supralabial scale. Belly varies from deep red to pale orange.

Habitat: Forests and moist woods, occasionally in pastures, bogs, and wet meadows, even in predominantly prairie counties.

Natural History: Active at ground level (during the day in spring and autumn, during night or twilight hours in summer), under rocks and logs, in rotting logs, and in piles of leaves; occasionally climbs into low shrubs. Emerges from hibernation in soil, gravel, rock crevices, etc., in March (during warm springs) and remains active into November. Mates May to September and 5–25 young (ca. 5–10 cm TL) are born August through early September. Earthworms and slugs make up most of the diet. Predators include snakes, birds, mammals, even large fish and frogs. Large numbers are killed on roads during spring and autumn as they move to and from upland hibernacula.

Status: Locally abundant, even in forested moraines of the Chicago region.

Redbelly snake (*Storeria occipitomaculata*), Cook Co., IL. (MR)
(Inset) Belly, McHenry Co., IL. (MR)

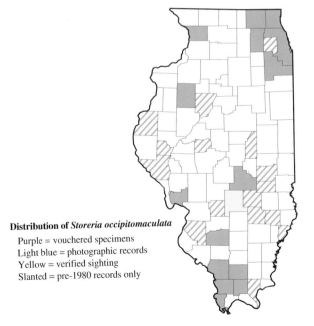

Distribution of *Storeria occipitomaculata*

Purple = vouchered specimens
Light blue = photographic records
Yellow = verified sighting
Slanted = pre-1980 records only

Flathead snake   **Colubridae**
Tantilla gracilis

Key Characters: Flattened head; minute eyes; back scales smooth and in 15 rows; anal plate divided.

Similar Species: Smooth earth snake, brown snake, redbelly snake.

Description: Diminutive (up to 20 cm TL) plain tan or yellow-brown snake with pointed head. Belly bright salmon or orange in the middle, becoming white toward the sides.

Habitat: Rocky, wooded limestone hillsides.

Natural History: Probably nocturnal and found mostly in spring and autumn under rocks, logs, and other moist debris in forest or brushy slopes. Burrows deeply as surface soil dries in summer. Sometimes found on or along roads at bottoms of rocky hillsides. Mates in April and May and deposits 2–4 eggs in moist soil or under rocks during June. Young hatch in September at 7–10 cm TL. Eats scorpions, spiders, centipedes, and a variety of other small arthropods, which it probably tracks by scent. Two small, grooved rear fangs and small venom glands are apparently used in subduing prey, but the snake is no threat to human beings and does not bite when handled. Preyed upon by birds, small mammals, lizards, and other snakes.

Status: Threatened in Illinois. Rare and localized along the southern Mississippi River bluffs.

Flathead snake (*Tantilla gracilis*), Oklahoma. (RWV)

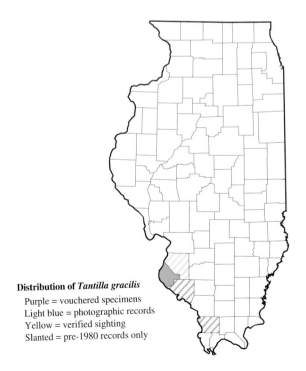

Distribution of *Tantilla gracilis*

Purple = vouchered specimens
Light blue = photographic records
Yellow = verified sighting
Slanted = pre-1980 records only

Western ribbon snake
Colubridae

Thamnophis proximus

Key Characteristics: Side stripe on scale rows 3–4; orange midback stripe; pair of light spots on top of the head; back scales keeled; anal plate not divided.

Similar Species: Eastern ribbon snake, common garter snake, plains garter snake.

Subspecies: Western ribbon snake, *T. p. proximus*.

Description: Medium-sized (up to 90 cm TL), slender black snake with an orange midback stripe and yellow or greenish stripes on each side. Belly greenish white. Tail about one-third of body length. Paired spots on top of head relatively large and partially fused. Usually 8 supralabial scales.

Habitat: Border vegetation around permanent bodies of water (swamps, marshes, ponds, rivers, ditches) and along bases of nearby rock outcrops where some individuals hibernate. Climbs onto piles of plants and low bushes.

Natural History: A quick, wary snake that climbs and swims readily. Bites when handled. Mates in April or May and gives birth to 10–15 young from July into October that are 15–20 cm TL. Diet mainly of fish and amphibians, especially frogs, and occasionally includes small reptiles. Among its predators are large shore birds, medium-sized mammals, and other snakes. Hibernates in rock crevices and burrows.

Status: Locally common along the Mississippi River valley and in southwestern counties, where cultivation and drainage of wetlands are major threats.

Western ribbon snake (*Thamnophis proximus*), Alexander Co., IL. (MR)

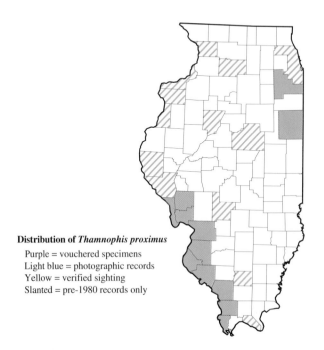

Distribution of *Thamnophis proximus*

Purple = vouchered specimens
Light blue = photographic records
Yellow = verified sighting
Slanted = pre-1980 records only

Plains garter snake
Thamnophis radix

Colubridae

Key Characters: Side stripes on scale rows 3–4; orange-yellow midback stripe; black bars on the margins of labial scales; back scales keeled; anal plate not divided.

Similar Species: Eastern ribbon snake, western ribbon snake, common garter snake, lined snake.

Subspecies: Eastern plains garter snake, *T. r. radix*.

Description: Medium-sized (up to 100 cm TL) dark brown or black snake with an orange-yellow midback strip and a yellow-gray stripe on each side. Two rows of alternating black spots or blotches on the side. Belly gray-green with dark spots along the edges. Usually a pair of light spots on top of the head.

Habitat: Former black-soil prairies, cultivated fields, pastures, wet meadows and marshes, and vacant lots.

Natural History: One of the most cold-tolerant snakes, often emerging from hibernation to bask on warm, sunny winter days. Mates in April or May and gives birth to 5–30 young from August through early October. Newborn 15–25 cm TL. Does not bite as readily as the common garter snake when handled. Common prey are earthworms, slugs, and small amphibians. Predators include birds of prey, mammals, and other snakes. Large numbers are killed on roads each spring and autumn as they move to and from upland hibernacula.

Status: Common in the northern half of the state.

Plains garter snake (*Thamnophis radix*), Cook Co., IL. (MR)

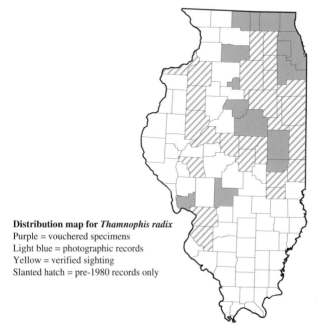

Distribution map for *Thamnophis radix*
Purple = vouchered specimens
Light blue = photographic records
Yellow = verified sighting
Slanted hatch = pre-1980 records only

Eastern ribbon snake

Colubridae

Thamnophis sauritus

Key Characteristics: Side stripes on scale rows 3–4; midback stripe yellow; if present, pair of spots on top of head faint and never touching each other; back scales keeled; anal plate not divided.

Similar Species: Western ribbon snake, common garter snake, plains garter snake.

Subspecies: Eastern ribbon snake, *T. s. sauritus*; northern ribbon snake, *T. s. septentrionalis*.

Description: Medium-sized (up to 80 cm TL), slender black snake with a yellow midback stripe and a yellow stripe on each side. A brown stripe on scale rows 1–2 extends onto the sides of belly scales. Remainder of belly plain greenish white. Two rows of black spots between back and side stripes. Long tail about one-third body length.

Habitat: Lowland forests, in vegetation along banks of sloughs, cypress-tupelo swamps, and other similar bodies of water.

Natural History: A quick, wary snake that moves to water, shoreline vegetation, or holes in the soil when disturbed. Mates in April or May and gives birth to 10–15 young between July and October. Amphibians make up most of the diet, but fish and invertebrates also eaten. Predators include wading birds, mammals, and other snakes.

Status: Endangered in Illinois. Known only from southeastern counties. Threats include drainage of swamplands and loss of aquatic and riparian vegetation.

Eastern ribbon snake (*Thamnophis sauritus*), Johnson Co., IL. (MR)

Distribution map for *Thamnophis sauritus*
Purple = vouchered specimens
Light blue = photographic records
Yellow = verified sighting
Slanted hatch = pre-1980 records only

Common garter snake
Thamnophis sirtalis

Colubridae

Key Characters: Side stripes on scale rows 2–3; yellow or gray midback stripe; black bars on margins of labial scales; back scales strongly keeled; anal scale not divided.

Similar Species: Eastern ribbon snake, western ribbon snake, plains garter snake, lined snake.

Subspecies: Chicago garter snake, *T. s. semifasciatus*; eastern garter snake, *T. s. sirtalis*.

Description: Medium-sized (up to 100 cm TL) dark brown or black snake with a yellow or gray midback stripe and a yellow stripe on each side. Belly gray-green with dark spots on edges of most belly scales. Head usually without parietal light spots. Some individuals have red coloring between side scales. In *T. s. semifasciatus*, the side stripe near the head is broken into a dashed line by black crossbars.

Habitat: Forests and edge habitats, commonly near water. Vacant lots in cities.

Natural History: Cold-tolerant snake that occasionally emerges from hibernation to bask on warm winter days. Mates immediately after emerging from hibernation, as early as March in southern counties. Females give birth to 15–80 young from July through early October that are 15–20 cm TL. Diet includes fish, amphibians, young birds, and a variety of invertebrates. Eaten by a wide variety of predatory vertebrates; people needlessly kill many.

Status: Common throughout the state.

Common garter snake (*Thamnophis sirtalis*), Saline Co., IL. (MR)

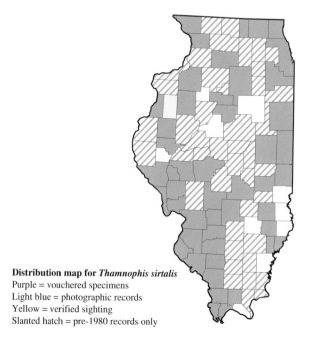

Distribution map for *Thamnophis sirtalis*
Purple = vouchered specimens
Light blue = photographic records
Yellow = verified sighting
Slanted hatch = pre-1980 records only

Lined snake   **Colubridae**
Tropidoclonion lineatum

Key Characteristics: White to gray midback stripe and another on each side; double row of dark half-moons extends down the midbelly; back scales keeled; anal plate not divided.

Similar Species: Common garter snake, plains garter snake.

Subspecies: Northern lined snake, *T. l. lineatum.*

Description: Small (up to 35 cm TL), slender olive brown to gray-brown snake. Each pale stripe is bordered by a row of minute black dots (dots more conspicuous in young). Head small, barely wider than body.

Habitat: Grasslands and urban lots in former prairie, where it is found under rocks, logs, leaves, boards, and other debris.

Natural History: Active March to November, spending less time at the surface during hot summers and more after heavy rains. Mates in late August and 5–10 young are born the following August or September. Newborn are 7–12 cm TL. This secretive and semifossorial nocturnal snake subsists almost entirely on earthworms. Predators include other snakes, birds, and mammals. Often curls its tail into a tight coil when disturbed, but otherwise passive.

Status: Rare and known from only a few scattered localities, mostly urban vacant lots, in central counties.

Lined snake (*Tropidoclonion lineatum*), Sangamon Co., IL. (MR)

Distribution map for *Tropidoclonion lineatum*
Purple = vouchered specimens
Light blue = photographic records
Yellow = verified sighting
Slanted hatch = pre-1980 records only

Smooth earth snake   **Colubridae**
Virginia valeriae

Key Characters: Back scales weakly keeled and in 17 rows; anal plate divided.

Similar Species: Ringneck snake, brown snake, redbelly snake, worm snake.

Subspecies: Western earth snake, *V. v. elegans*.

Description: Small (up to 35 cm TL), medium brown, dark olive, or gray-brown snake with a distinct head and plain white belly. Back unpatterned (sometimes with minute dark flecks). Belly white, usually with a slight greenish yellow tint, sometimes with a few dark flecks toward the side. Pointed snout.

Habitat: Rocky, wooded hillsides.

Natural History: Semifossorial and nocturnal. Surface activity sometimes stimulated by heavy rains. Often found in or under rotting logs, as well as under rocks and in forest-floor leaf litter. Mates late April or May, after emerging from hibernation in deep hillside crevices, and 3–8 tiny young are born in August. Newborn 7–12 cm TL and may be darker than adults. Diet includes mainly earthworms and other soft-bodied insects, slugs, and snails. Predators include other snakes, birds, and mammals.

Status: Locally common in the Shawnee Hills (Fig. 1) and the bluffs along the Mississippi River in southern counties.

Smooth earth snake (*Virginia valeriae*), Jackson Co., IL. (MR)

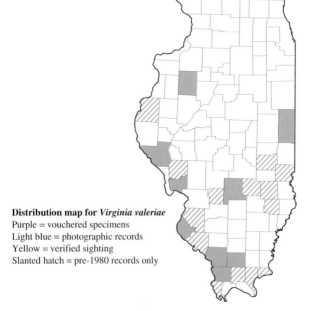

Distribution map for *Virginia valeriae*
Purple = vouchered specimens
Light blue = photographic records
Yellow = verified sighting
Slanted hatch = pre-1980 records only

VENOMOUS

Copperhead
Agkistrodon contortrix

Viperidae

Key Characters: Nine large symmetrical plates on top of head; elliptical pupil; pit between eye and nostril; back with hourglass-shaped crossbands; back scales strongly keeled; anal plate not divided.

Similar Species: Cottonmouth, fox snake, northern water snake.

Subspecies: Northern copperhead, *A. c. mokasen*; and intergradation between northern and southern copperhead, *A. c. contortrix.*

Description: Large (up to 135 cm TL), stout-bodied venomous snake. Back yellowish brown or rusty brown with 10–20 reddish brown hourglass-shaped, dark-margined crossbands that are narrow across the back and wider on the sides. Belly yellow to brown with brown blotches near the edges. Top of head red-brown. Thin dark line extends from eye to angle of jaw. The sulfur yellow tail tip of newborn darkens with maturity.

Habitat: Wooded, rocky hillsides and forest edges, sometimes in meadows and fields during summer.

Natural History: This shy snake is active April through October. Often seen around old, abandoned buildings where it feeds on rodents. Mates in April and May or September and October. Three to 10 young, 20–25 cm TL, are born in late August or early September. Predators include other snakes, birds of prey, and medium-sized mammals.

Status: Although probably reduced by habitat destruction and wanton killing by people, it remains locally abundant in the Shawnee Hills and the bluffs along the southern Mississippi River.

Copperhead (*Agkistrodon contortrix*), Jackson Co., IL. (MR)

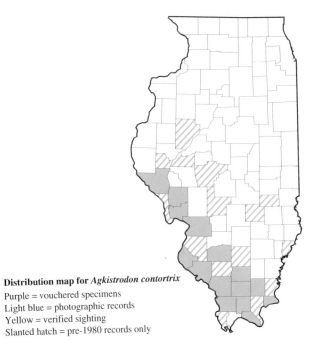

Distribution map for *Agkistrodon contortrix*

Purple = vouchered specimens
Light blue = photographic records
Yellow = verified sighting
Slanted hatch = pre-1980 records only

VENOMOUS

Cottonmouth
Viperidae
Agkistrodon piscivorus

Key Characters: Nine large symmetrical plates on top of head; elliptical pupil; pit between eye and nostril; back uniformly black or with ragged dark crossbands; back scales strongly keeled; anal plate not divided.

Similar Species: Copperhead, northern water snake, Mississippi green water snake.

Subspecies: Western cottonmouth, *A. p. leucostoma*.

Description: Large (up to 159 cm TL), stout-bodied venomous snake. Juveniles and young adults have 12–18 dark crossbands on an olive or dark brown back and a dark stripe from snout through eye and upper lip. With age, adults become uniformly dark olive or black. Belly tan to gray and heavily marked with black. The sulfur yellow tail tip of newborn darkens with maturity.

Habitat: Cypress-tupelo swamps, sloughs, and oxbow lakes of extreme southern counties.

Natural History: Active April through October, often sunning on logs extending into water. When threatened, the mouth is opened in an exaggerated manner to expose the starkly contrasting white mouth lining. Opportunistic predators of fish, amphibians, other reptiles, and small mammals. Three to eight young born in late August or early September. Newborn 20–30 cm TL. Adults have few enemies other than human beings, but young are eaten by large fish, snapping turtles, other snakes, wading birds, and mammals.

Status: Has declined with draining and clearing of bottomland swamps and sloughs, but remains abundant in relatively undisturbed habitats.

Cottonmouth (*Agkistrodon piscivorus*), Pope Co., IL. (MR)

Distribution map for *Agkistrodon piscivorus*
Purple = vouchered specimens
Light blue = photographic records
Yellow = verified sighting
Slanted hatch = pre-1980 records only

VENOMOUS

Massasauga   Viperidae
Sistrurus catenatus

Key Characters: Nine large symmetrical plates on top of head; elliptical pupil; pit between eye and nostril; light-edged dark blotches on back and sides; rattle or horny button on tail tip; 4 head stripes; back scales strongly keeled; anal plate not divided.

Similar Species: Timber rattlesnake, fox snake.

Subspecies: Eastern massasauga, *S. c. catenatus.*

Description: Medium-sized (up to 100 cm TL) venomous snake. Back gray to light brown with 29–40 light-edged dark brown or black blotches down the middle. Three rows of smaller, alternating dark blotches along each side. One black head stripe behind each pit, two on top. Belly black with irregular white or yellow markings. Newborn tail tip yellow, but darkens with age.

Habitat: Old fields, floodplain forests, marshlands, and bogs.

Natural History: Active April through October, often suns on clumps of grass, in branches of small shrubs, or near crayfish burrows. Feeds on small rodents. Breeds spring and autumn with 4–20 young born late summer or early autumn. Newborn 20–30 cm TL. Main predators are hawks, predatory mammals, and other snakes.

Status: Endangered in Illinois. Formerly common over northern two-thirds of the state, prior to drainage of prairie marshes and intensive agriculture. Once known from 24 widely scattered relict populations, now thought to occur at only 6-8.

Massasauga (*Sistrurus catenatus*), Clinton Co., IL. (SB)

Distribution map for *Sistrurus catenatus*
Purple = vouchered specimens
Light blue = photographic records
Yellow = verified sighting
Slanted hatch = pre-1980 records only

VENOMOUS

Timber rattlesnake   **Viperidae**
Crotalus horridus

Key Characters: Small asymmetrical head scales; elliptical pupil; pit between eye and nostril; back with jagged dark bands; rattle or button on tail tip; back scales strongly keeled; anal scale not divided.

Similar Species: Massasauga.

Description: Large (up to 180 cm TL), stout-bodied venomous snake. Back gray, light yellow, or greenish white with 20–25 black, jagged crossbars or blotches. Sometimes an orange or rust stripe down midback. Head clearly larger than slender neck. Dark stripe behind each eye. Tail tip uniformly black in adults. Belly pink, white, cream, or gray, with dark stippling toward sides.

Habitat: Heavy forest along rocky outcrops and bluffs.

Natural History: Active April through October, often seen sunning on rock ledges near winter dens. Forages during summer in upland forests and some border and disturbed habitats where rodents are abundant. Diet mainly small mammals, such as mice, squirrels, and chipmunks. Usually mates July and August with 6–10 young born late summer or early autumn of following year. Newborn 25–35 cm TL. Predators of young include hawks, coyotes, skunks, foxes, and common kingsnakes. Most adult mortality caused by vehicles and wanton killing by humans.

Status: Threatened in Illinois. Previously more widespread, now probably occurs in moderate numbers only in the Shawnee Hills (Fig. 1). Relict elsewhere. Threats, besides indiscriminate killing by people, include vehicles and clearing of forest.

Timber rattlesnake (*Crotalus horridus*), Union Co., IL. (SB)

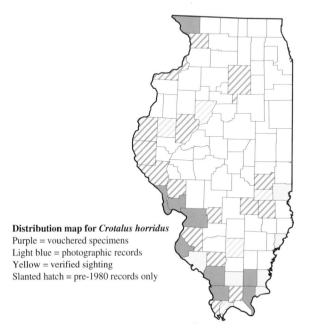

Distribution map for *Crotalus horridus*
Purple = vouchered specimens
Light blue = photographic records
Yellow = verified sighting
Slanted hatch = pre-1980 records only

Species of Questionable Occurrence in Illinois

Tremblay's salamander   *Ambystoma tremblayi*

This unisexual member of the *A. jeffersonianum* complex was accidentally introduced to a pond in Cook County in the late 1970s. Recent surveys indicate that this all-female species has colonized neighboring ponds.

Three-toed box turtle   *Terrapene carolina triungus*

This subspecies of the common box turtle is not considered native to Illinois. Over the last several years four individuals have been captured along the Mississippi River in western Illinois. Because the three-toed box turtle is an inhabitant of adjacent Missouri, these individuals may have crossed the river by swimming or during flood events. It is also possible that they were introduced into Illinois by humans.

Scarlet snake   *Cemophora coccinea*

The only specimen of this species from Illinois was collected by F.R. Cagle at Wolf Lake Swamp in Union County. It was originally cataloged as *Lampropeltis triangulum syspila*, but later identified as *Cemophora coccinea* by Philip Smith, noted herpetologist at the Illinois Natural History Survey. Repeated searching of Wolf Lake and the slopes of adjacent Pine Hills Recreation Area has not yielded any additional specimens. Phil Smith accepted the record as valid, based mainly on similar isolated records for this species in Indiana and Missouri.

Additional Reading

Ballard, S.R. 1996. Don't let these snakes rattle you!! Illinois Audubon, Spring 1996 (256):4-7.

Ballard, S.R. 1994. Threatened and endangered Illinois herpetofauna. The Illinois Steward 3(3):23-26.

Brandon, R.A., and S.R. Ballard. 1996. Are frogs, toads and salamanders declining in Illinois? Illinois Audubon, Winter 1996-97 (259):4-9.

Conant, R., and J.T. Collins. 1991. A field guide to reptiles and amphibians of eastern and central North America [Peterson field guide series]. 3d ed. Houghton Mifflin Co., Boston & New York. xx + 450 pp.

Dreslik, M.J, E.O. Moll, C.A. Phillips, and T.P. Wilson. 1997. The endangered and threatened turtles of Illinois. Illinois Audubon, Winter 1997-98 (263):10-15.

Garman, H. 1892. A synopsis of the reptiles and amphibians of Illinois. Illinois Laboratory of Natural History Bulletin 3(13):215-388.

Johnson, T.R. 1987. The amphibians and reptiles of Missouri. Missouri Department of Conservation, Jefferson City. 368 pp.

Lueth, F.X. 1941. Manual of Illinois snakes. Illinois Department of Conservation, Springfield. 48 pp.

Minton, S.A. 1972. Amphibians and reptiles of Indiana. Indiana Academy of Science Monograph No. 3:1-346.

Moll, E.O. 1997. Illinois' yellow mud turtle. The Illinois Steward 6(1):16-19.

O'Donnell, D.J. 1937. Natural history of the ambystomatid salamanders of Illinois. American Midland Naturalist 18:1063-1071.

Parmalee, P.A. 1954. Amphibians of Illinois. Illinois State Museum Story of Illinois Series 10:38.

Parmalee, P.A. 1955. Reptiles of Illinois. Illinois State Museum Popular Science Series 5:88.

Phillips, C.A., and H. Korab. 1998. Eastern massasauga: a rare rattlesnake in Illinois. The Illinois Steward 7(3):2-6.

Smith, P.W. 1947. The reptiles and amphibians of east central Illinois. Bulletin of the Chicago Academy of Sciences 8(2):21-40.

Smith, P.W. 1961. The amphibians and reptiles of Illinois. Illinois Natural History Survey Bulletin 28:1-298.

Vogt, R.C. 1981. Natural history of amphibians and reptiles in Wisconsin. The Milwaukee Public Museum. 205 pp.

Index of Common and Scientific Names